A Moon
on
Water

A Moon on Water

Activities, Games and Stories for Developing Children's Spiritual Intelligence

Roy Leighton, Trisha Lee,
Tim Harding and Steve Bowkett

Crown House Publishing Ltd
www.crownhouse.co.uk
www.crownhousepublishing.com

First published by
Crown House Publishing Ltd
Crown Buildings, Bancyfelin, Carmarthen, Wales, SA33 5ND, UK
www.crownhouse.co.uk
and
Crown House Publishing Company LLC
6 Trowbridge Drive, Suite 5, Bethel, CT 06801, USA
www.crownhousepublishing.com

British Library of Cataloguing-in-Publication Data
A catalogue entry for this book is available
from the British Library.

10-digit ISBN 184590392-7
13-digit ISBN 978-184590392-3

LCCN 2009936672

Printed and bound in the UK by
Bell & Bain Ltd, Glasgow

To the visionary Japanese educationalist Tsunesaburo Makiguchi (1872 – 1944). Your thinking and selfless example has shaped my life and work in more ways than I can list here. With my sincere gratitude. Nam-Myoho-Renge-Kyo.

Roy Leighton

To my sister, Lors, for lying in the bed next to mine when we were both children and spending her nights telling me stories explaining how a simple coloured stone got all its marks and enabling me to find a sense of spirituality in the simplest of things.

Trisha Lee

To all those who I have taught – and who have, in turn, taught me.

Tim Harding

To Alan Watts who pointed at the moon, and to Little Cat and friends for the lessons they teach.

Steve Bowkett

Contents

How to use this book
   This delightful book contains stories, activities, music and worksheets to be mixed and matched to create your own lessons. There are two CDs in the back of the book, the audio CD contains stories from the book with accompanying music. The resources CD contains the printable resources for classroom activities. We have indicated the relevant tracks and filenames in the Contents listing below.

Activities:

Foreword by
Dr David George

This fascinating book helps you put spirituality into the curriculum through the medium of a wide variety of stories suitable for all ages.

The nature of spiritual intelligence is difficult to define. One point to make clear is that it is quite separate from organised religion. Spirituality is about questions more than answers and lives in stories, poetry, metaphor, uncertainty and paradox. All these are evident in this thought-provoking book.

One of the qualities of spirituality is wisdom and this includes knowing the limits of your knowledge. Other ingredients are values such as courage, integrity and compassion. Spirituality means more is less rather than less is more so as you learn, the process may involve unlearning what others may have taught you. Spirituality is an essential component of a holistic approach to life and work, it finds expression in creativity and all forms of the Arts. It is the 'glue' that holds together our conscious intellect and our intelligent action.

In a holistic view of life we are people with a mind, a body and a spirit all interconnected and arranged in a pattern that means that the whole is greater than the sum of the parts. This book advocates the education of the whole child, as the head, heart and hand all need educating.

The book is a fund of stories, both traditional and original from different cultures and belief systems, which are so relevant to our multi ethnic society, and is accompanied by an excellent CD with further stories and appropriate music. In order to get the best from this book teachers and parents should read the introduction, which gives an overview and describes the intentions of the authors.

Written with compassion, humanity and with the humour in which children revel, these stories make excellent starting points for discussion in Circle Time, PHSE, Religious Studies as well as School Assemblies. Such discussions can help children consider the problems which face the world today and form a great starting point for considering the nature of beliefs and values and the way in which they contribute to any ethical stance we make.

In this age of uncertainty, when changing events and situations appear to be beyond our control, children need to be able to develop their inner strength so they can adapt rather than give up or give in. Spirituality sustains us from within when all else falls away. We use our spiritual intelligence to dream, to aspire and to raise ourselves up.

I am pleased to commend this book to all parents and teachers. It makes a magical read.

Dr David George, Northampton

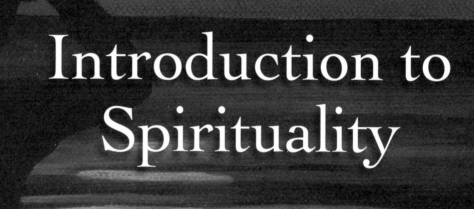

Introduction to Spirituality

Introduction

Our personal views on spirituality

Roy Leighton

Steve, Trish, Tim and I are prefacing this book by briefly setting out what spirituality means to each of us. The primary purpose for this is to highlight that although we may all have significantly different 'vehicles' that serve to transport us individually throughout this life there are common elements of spirituality that go beyond individuals and the organisations they may choose to use to explore a spiritual life. Indeed, in my own case, I have looked at a number of spiritual and religious methodologies before settling, over twenty-five years ago, with Buddhism as my chosen system for exploring both the mysteries and certainties that are contained within a spiritual existence.

Whilst I am very comfortable with being a practising Buddhist and part of SGI-UK and SGI (the national and global family of Buddhists), I loathe the idea that being part of an organisation suggests that I have chosen to suppress my sense of self. I am very disturbed by the closed actions of those (of any faith) who seek to reassure themselves that they have found 'the way' or 'nirvana' by seeking to convert everyone to their own spiritual journey.

Too many of my negative experiences of spirituality take the form of being cornered by very committed individuals with a strong faith in their own beliefs who lacked the tact, sensitivity, respect or capacity to appreciate that the path they have chosen was not, necessarily, the right path for everyone. I have to confess that in the early years of my Buddhist practice I felt it was my 'mission' to convert others to the true faith. This was until an older Buddhist with a deeper understanding of Buddhism and life made it perfectly clear that to seek to undermine someone else's belief only serves to highlight the lack of depth, understanding and faith in one's own religious practice. His advice was to attend to my own 'human revolution' and leave others to do the same.

Therefore I write this introduction in order to celebrate the struggles and revelations of all those engaged in a genuine endeavour to understand the essence of spirituality. I do not believe that a spiritual path is anything other than a desire to discover and apply fundamental laws that are true, practical and of assistance on a daily basis. Whatever religious or spiritual practice we may find ourselves attached to it is the search for truth, and then to live that truth, that is our challenge. Indeed, the truth and the search for truth is the driving force for all those intent on understanding themselves and their role in this world. The ninth century Islamic scholar Abu Yusuf Al Kindi (801–873) summed this up beautifully when he said: 'We should not shy away from welcoming and acquiring the truth regardless of where it comes from, even if it comes from distant races and nations that are different from us. Nothing is more important than seeking the truth except the truth itself.'

You do not need to be 'religious' to be spiritual. For example, scientists, legal professionals and teachers whilst not necessarily being of a religious bent have chosen professions that require a constant assessment and readjustment of their thinking and actions. With that search for truth comes the logical deduction that as new understandings and deeper truths reveal themselves then our thinking, actions and interactions will change. This means that we will, over time and with new experiences, change as well. This is logical not mystical, and what my wiser Buddhist friend referred to as doing our 'human revolution'.

For me Buddhism provides a system that enables me to engage practically in this exploration of the spiritual. So, to conclude, I follow the teachings of the thirteenth century Japanese Buddha Nichiren Daishonin (1222–1282). I seek to create the space twice a day to stop, reflect and recite from the Lotus Sutra to prepare for and then reflect on my day.

The benefits of these regular moments of prayer and reflection have, over the years, provided me with space to re-think and re-act. In particular the power of creating these dynamic daily sessions of stillness have assisted, in a very practical way, to my contribution to this book.

On Spirituality and Me

Trish Lee

Spirituality is the word that best anchors the uncertainty of my beliefs. I am not able to declare that I follow a particular religion, neither on the other hand am I able to proclaim myself agnostic.

But I do hold a strong sense of spirituality.

When sixteen years ago, I first held my newborn son in my arms and looked at his tiny fingers, I felt an abundant connection with the essence of life.

When ten years ago, I was first privileged to listen to children inventing stories that sought to answer universal questions, I felt that same propensity ignite in me.

When I drove home yesterday, to be chased by a rainbow, I got out of my car and walked for a while, just to look up to the heavens and feel invigorated by the rain on my face.

As a child I had plenty of religious input. I attended a Roman Catholic primary school that was also a convent. As one of only a handful of non-baptised children, the nuns struggled to know what to do with me; particularly when the rest of the class were studying towards their Holy Communion. I remember watching in envy as the girls in my class arrived wearing beautiful white dresses, and walked proudly to the altar to experience their first Eucharist, whilst I sat at the back of the church out of the way of their parents.

My evening and weekends were filled with Sunday school, Bible Class and Monday Nighters at the local Gospel Chapel, and I was brought up on a mixture of Hail Mary's, lengthy sermons and readings from the scriptures. My party piece till the age of 11 was reciting the books of the Old Testament in order.

But then it changed; a comprehensive secondary school meant that all that remained of my highly religious primary experience was being top of the class in RE and carrying a constant sense of culpability whenever anything went wrong.

As I grew older I began to question the sense of guilt that still clings to me today; and that many who know me ascribe to my Catholic past.

But although I moved away from organised religion, midnight mass and nightly prayers, I never quite moved away from the sense of wonder that the world inspires in me; from my need to ask questions and search for the answers, to know what it all means.

It is this fundamental necessity to search out what is unfathomable that I define as the root of my spirituality.

Spirituality: A Religious Experience?

Tim Harding

Spirituality is that human dimension which involves personal thought, wonderment and questioning: the capacity to search for understanding, seek meaning and make sense both of ourselves and the things that surround us. Such thinking can lead to belief, trust and faith.

My own faith background has been within the context of English Anglicanism – as a life-long church member, and for some of my career, a teacher and head teacher in Church of England schools.

For me, the beauty, nature and purpose of God is seen in the world and the people around us, and religion gives us a spiritual vocabulary and frameworks which help us to search for, develop and perhaps recognise our own personal faith, belief and spirituality. However, personal spirituality is present in all of us, whether or not we link this to religious belief. It is an aspect of ourselves that we can all develop, and that we can help others to develop too in order to enhance our life experience.

As an educator my priority has always been to provide the greatest channels of opportunity possible for the development of the child – in any area, be it academic, creative, physical or emotional/spiritual.

In all of these areas there is a responsibility to guide, encourage and nurture, recognising strengths and weaknesses, but underpinning all these is the responsibility to respect the personal spirituality of the individual. In our guidance, the ability to influence and steer this spirituality must be governed and restrained by respect for the views of the children we are teaching.

My hope is that this book will provide many opportunities for the development and encouragement of children's spiritual intelligence, stimulating thought and discussion, perhaps even providing some enlightenment and answers.

Going Myself

Steve Bowkett

Albert Einstein once said: 'There are two ways to live your life. One is as though nothing is a miracle. The other is as though everything is a miracle.' Bearing in mind that the origin of the word miracle is 'to wonder at' (and is linked through Old English and Sanskrit to 'we smile'), I think this is a good standpoint to take as I consider the spiritual aspect of my personality.

Wonderment is one of a number of feelings we can have in the face of ignorance and unknowing. Frustration is another, doubt and denial two more. Or maybe I should qualify that by saying that these feelings arise as we *engage* with what is unknown: it is easy enough never to bother to think about such matters, in which case – to quote the beautiful and horrifying words of poet Vachel Lindsay – we 'die like sheep'. Wonderment is more of a verb-process than it is a noun-state. I believe that to wonder lies at the heart of spirituality – mine anyway – and is one of the cornerstones of any attempts we make to cultivate 'spiritual intelligence' in others.

So out of the wondering I've done so far, where do I stand in all of this? I think that the astonishing nature and fruitfulness of the universe is not an accident and that it is pregnant with meaning and purpose. Since I am embedded in that universe as an integral part of it, my existence and what I make of it is filled also with meaning and purpose. Sometimes I feel the sense of the guidance of a personal God; providing as it were flexibility within the structure of the manifested world – a feeling of living (as I think Marcel Proust said) 'an authored life'. While these beliefs lie at the heart of Christianity (and are beautifully explored in the books of John Polkinghorne) I wouldn't necessarily call myself a Christian or in fact a subscriber to any organised religion.

I am also intrigued by the Hindu concept of the cosmos as a kind of dance, a thing of organic elegance rather than the blind and purposeless machine metaphor so beloved by many modern atheists. For me the cosmic dance is consonant with the image, originating in the Mahayana Buddhist tradition, of Indra's net. The philosopher Alan Watts imagines this as being like a dew-covered cobweb on a sunny morning, where each drop of dew contains the reflection of all the other drops. But I have a feeling that these sparkling drops, like eyes, are looking at each other. I think that the universe is self-aware – which means that consciousness is bundled up as an essential part of the whole thing, and may be as fundamental as the other elements of spacetime for anything to exist. The main implication of this for me is that what I think and how I use my life has a significance in the bigger picture of everything that is going on. I am a participant in the dance and how I move counts.

One of the most elegant recent discussions of these ideas (and many more) is to be found in psychologist Dean Radin's book *The Conscious Universe*. Here he addresses the big questions of both science and to some extent religion, and attempts to resolve the divide that has opened up between them. Personally I think there need be no conflict between what science is trying to achieve or can ultimately discover, and the fact that human beings undeniably have a spiritual aspect to their personalities. But I also think it is wise, however we make our way, to bear in mind the old wisdom that the opposite of faith is not doubt, but certainty.

Endeavouring to Make Sense of What We Don't Understand

Stories

Tales to Tell

Key idea:
How stories and quotes act as springboards into further thinking and discussion.

One day the Minister of State for Education decided to find out how teachers could best help children to develop their spiritual intelligence. He assembled his wisest advisors and then drew a line on a large sheet of paper laid out on the table. He said, 'Whoever can make the line longer without touching it will be fit for purpose in drafting the Government's new policy document on this matter!'

Advisor after advisor stepped up to the line and scratched their heads over this impossible puzzle. The last advisor had brought her 7-year-old daughter with her to Parliament this day, because the childminder had fallen ill. Before anyone could stop her, the young girl snatched up a marker pen and drew a second, shorter line parallel to the first. She was immediately given the job.

Stories and quotes are a great way to show children the kind of attitude that raises spiritual awareness. Such an attitude is a delightful blend of creativity, fun, curiosity, enthusiasm, determination and independence of judgement.

Emperor: *Priest, I am worried about what happens to my soul after I die. Tell me please.*

Priest: *How should I know?*

Emperor: *Why, because you're a man of God!*

Priest: *Yes master, but not a dead one yet.*

A blackbird found a tasty scrap of food on a village street one day and, snatching it up, flew towards the clouds. He was immediately set upon by a gang of crows, who harried him until he released the morsel.

They flew off fighting noisily over the titbit. 'Well,' thought the blackbird, 'I may have lost the food, but I have regained the peace of this endless sky.'

When you are full of doubt, even a thousand books of scripture are not enough. When you understand, even one word is too much.

Fen Yang

The nature of God is a circle of which the centre is everywhere and the circumference is nowhere.

Empedocles

It is not the same to talk of bulls as it is to be in the bullring.

Spanish proverb

Lift the stone and you will find me. Cleave the wood and I am there.

Jesus

Set up a quotes board in the classroom where you and the children can post sayings that have taught you, puzzled you, moved you or made you laugh.

To do:

■ Tell 'stories of the spirit' often. Take time to discuss them with the class. What lessons do we learn? How can we apply them in our lives?

■ Retell traditional tales of wisdom and put them in a contemporary context. Can such stories be linked to modern problems – global warming, the threat of terrorism, Third World poverty, the destruction of the rain forests? Or encourage the children to write new stories suggesting solutions.

I threw my cup away when I saw a child drinking from the trough.

Diogenes

Saying Goodbye

Key ideas:

Sometimes the problems that we have to face in life can seem too big, too painful – and to make no sense. Yet often the simplest statement from the most unexpected source can bring the greatest insight …

The shock Dawn felt was far greater than she'd anticipated. For three years her mother had moved slowly and inevitably towards death – in the last few moments death had arrived. Her mother lay still and silent in the hospice bed, her journey finally over.

Dawn began to cry. Her sobs were a marriage of relief and rage. She was now, at the age of 41, suddenly an orphan. Her father had passed away seven years before and the pain of that passing now returned and added to this new loss. As her sobs subsided, Dawn sat on the bed, gently moving the wisps of hair that had fallen across her mother's face.

'She's gone. I am sorry.' The voice of the nurse, although soft and genuinely concerned, seemed somewhat out of place in this space; this tiny moment in time, between being and not being. 'I'll be just outside. Take as long as you need and come and fetch me if and when you need me. I'm so sorry, she was a lovely woman.'

Was? So quickly from being 'is' to 'was', thought Dawn.

After some time sitting with her silent disbelief, Dawn suddenly rose. She carefully placed her mother's hand back on the bed, kissed her forehead and took a deep breath, 'I'd better call home.'

The phone call was not one that Dawn wanted to make. Andy, her husband, would be getting the girls ready for school. Her girls. Dawn began to cry again, now not for her mother, but for her children.

How would they deal with the loss of Nanny, who had lived so close to them all their lives? She'd even moved in with them seven years ago after the death of her husband, Dawn's dad and their grandfather (or 'Pap' as he was affectionately known).

Quite simply, Nanny had always been there. She'd shared so many moments, from bath-times to holidays, birthdays to Christmases. She had been there when Zoe, now 11, had taken her first steps. She'd recently passed on the mysteries of knitting to 9-year-old Becky who had produced a rather splendid scarf for her father. She had shared in the delights and joyful mess of 6-year-old Ruby's first attempts at cake making. She was (that word again) too much part of the family for them not to be forever changed and shifted by her loss.

The phone call made, Dawn waited – and worried. How would they cope? What would they do when they saw Nanny? Would they *want* to see her?

After a short while, Andy and the girls arrived at the ward. It was clear that Zoe and Becky had been crying. Andy, too, showed signs of recent weeping but Ruby was running to investigate the huge aquarium by the nurses' station.

'Dad, look! A blue fish! It's huge!' cried Ruby.

Zoe and Becky joined Ruby to look at the fish.

Dawn heard the girls' excited voices and came out of the room where she had spent the past hour in silence with her mother.

On seeing her lively, beautiful daughters, Dawn burst into tears. They ran to her and surrounded her with a warm, loving fence of arms and held on to her tightly. Andy walked over to his gaggle of girls and kissed Dawn.

'You okay?' he asked.

'Not really,' said Dawn, putting her arms around Andy's neck and pulling him to her.

After a short while, the girls were asked if they'd like to say goodbye to Nanny. They all said they wanted to and were taken into the room where they stood at the end of the bed staring at their grandmother.

'She looks like she's sleeping.'

'Well, she is, sort of.'

'Can we touch her?'

'Yes – go and say goodbye.'

The children walked to the side of the bed and whispered their farewells into Nanny's ear and gently kissed her forehead, as she had done so many times to them.

'Can we go and look at the garden?' Becky asked.

'Of course,' said Dawn.

'We'll keep the noise down!' assured Zoe, as they walked towards the door.

As the girls left, Ruby suddenly turned and ran back to her mum. She hugged Dawn and looked up at her. 'Nanny is happy now. She's going to be with Pap and that's what she wanted more than anything, because he's been waiting for seven years and now they're going to be together – and that's good.'

'Yes, my love,' said Dawn, tears in her eyes.

'Nanny just wanted to make sure we were OK before she left.'

'She did, darling.'

'And we are OK, aren't we Mum?'

Dawn paused and looked lovingly at the wise and wonderful child in front of her. 'Yes, darling. We are.'

'We're just sad. And we all get sad sometimes.'

'That's right darling. We're just sad.'

With that, Ruby smiled up at Dawn, turned and ran off to join her sisters in the garden.

To do:

■ Ask the children what they would say or do to support someone who is dealing with the loss of someone that they loved. What would they like people to say and do to support them?

■ For an older group of children (10 and above) ask them if they have had to deal with the loss of someone. How did they feel? What was the reaction of the adults around them? How do they feel now?

■ Ask the children to draw an image of where they think people go to when they die. Once they have completed the drawings ask them to describe what they have drawn and why? Develop this as appropriate to the maturity and age of the children.

Take it further:

■ Why are some people frightened of dying?

■ Can the death of a pet be as important to a child as the death of an adult?

■ The story suggests that often children deal with death and dying with greater acceptance than adults. Why might this be the case?

■ Would it have been better in the story for the children not to have said goodbye to their grandmother?

Koan, Koan – Gone!

Key ideas:

Sometimes 'spiritual understanding' isn't something that can be reasoned out or reached through intellectual effort. Stories are often powerful in helping us to understand in both a reasoned and intuitive way.

For thousands of years human beings have tried to go beyond the ordinary and mundane in search of the transcendent. We look for clues and signs to assure us that there is something other than our physical existence in time and space; that our lives and the universe we live in amount to more than a random dance of atoms without any further meaning attached to them. Certainly in recent times, perhaps since the Renaissance, the rise of science and logical thought has added immensely to our understanding of the cosmos and of ourselves. And yet reason per se seems to have achieved little in satisfying the spiritual need that exists in most if not all of us. We have not been able to analyse our way to enlightenment.

A koan is a story, question or statement arising out of the Zen tradition. It is usually enigmatic or paradoxical and is designed to confound the rational analytical mind so that it *gives up trying* to solve the puzzle. Koan may also surprise or shock the listener into sudden insight, or serve more formally as a 'teaching tale'.

One of the most famous koans is: *What is the sound of one hand clapping?* Immediately we try to think about it, to work it out – and get nowhere. Any answer might well be inadequate.

Another famous story concerns the Japanese master Nan-in who was visited by a university professor wishing to learn about Zen. They took tea together and Nan-in filled the professor's cup to the brim and then continued pouring. 'What are you doing?' the professor complained, 'No more will go in!' Nan-in replied, 'You are like this cup, full of your own opinions and speculations. Empty yourself of them, and then you can learn.'

Elsewhere the wanderer Dojen was confronted by the Emperor: 'You seem to be very contented with your life, Dojen. What is the secret of your happiness?' At this Dojen laid down the bundle he was carrying. The Emperor realised that somehow this was very wise. He said, 'I see. And how may I find such serenity?' Dojen picked up his bundle and went on his way.

Another parable tells of a traveller who encountered a tiger. He fled and the tiger chased him. Soon he came to the edge of a cliff and swung himself over by grabbing at a wild vine. Looking down, the traveller saw the tiger's mate waiting below. Just as the vine started to tear loose, the traveller saw a ripe strawberry growing just within arm's reach and in his last moments picked it and put it to his lips. How sweet it tasted!

The philosopher Alan Watts tells us that *this is it!* This is all of life – the present moment and our ordinary experience of it, and by simply appreciating life our spiritual needs are satisfied and a greater meaning reveals itself.

Links:

Paul Reps' *Zen Flesh, Zen Bones*, Steve Bowkett's *Dojen the Wanderer* and *For the Moon There is the Cloud*.

To do:

■ Read the koan above, or the stories elsewhere in the book (or of course from other sources) to the class. Ask the children *how* they make sense of these stories. Are they trying to think them out logically? If that works, what do the stories reveal to our common sense way of thinking? If the stories seem to be nonsensical, what emotional reactions do the children have to them?

■ In some Eastern spiritual traditions the sacred is expressed in terms of the ordinary and everyday. Put the idea to the group that if God (or any answer to our big question 'What's it all about?') could be found right here, now, where we are – how would the children realise it? And how would they talk about it?

Link:

R. S. Thomas's poem 'The View from the Window' offers a beautiful example of what I mean.

When we went to say goodbye to my Mother at the chapel of rest after she died my brother ran out of the room and came back with a conker he'd found on the ground and clasped it into her hand. Knowing she's underground now with the warmth of a smooth brown conker helps me to handle missing her.

Tab Neal

The Harp of Dagda

Key ideas:

Different elements of music such as speed, instrumentation and style can create an emotional response in us. Listening to music can make us laugh, motivate us into action, soothe and calm, or even move us to tears.

Ancient writings from Ireland tell stories of some of the first peoples to live in that country: the dark-haired giants – called Formorians – and the fair-haired, fair-skinned Tuatha de Danaan, who possessed magical powers. One of the greatest warriors and heroes of the Tuatha de Danaan was the Dagda – the Good God. Music was very important in ancient Ireland, and the Dagda had a magical harp – sometimes played by a harpist and sometimes by the Dagda himself. It was an old harp, carved from oak and studded with jewels. But during the second battle of Moytura the harp was captured by the Formorians and taken back to their camp.

Dagda and two companions Lugh and Ogma made their way to the Formorians' camp.

Creeping into the hall of the castle where the giants were feasting, the Dagda saw his harp hanging on the wall.

And then in a loud voice he cried out:

19

'Come to me, Oak of two greens

Come to me four-angled music! Come summer, Come winter!

Mouths of harps and bags and pipes!'

The harp flew across the room, striking Formorian warriors on its way – nine men were killed by that harp. And then the Dagda caught the harp and began to play the three noble types of tune played in Ireland in those days.

First he played *goltrai*: crying music, which was so sad that soon all were in tears. Next he played *geantrai*: the music of laughter. Forgetting their sadness, the Formorians became wild with laughter and silliness. Finally he played *suantrai*: the music of sleep, which was so calm and soothing that everyone fell into a deep slumber.

And the Dagda and his companions escaped into the night with the magic harp.

To do:

■ Can you think of at least two songs or pieces of music that make you feel: sad/happy and excited/relaxed or sleepy?

■ What is it about them that produces this effect? Is it the instruments that are playing, the rhythm, the speed, the words or the way it is being played?

■ If you were writing a piece of music for one of these responses, what would you include? This could be developed into creative music making.

■ Complete the worksheet to list your feelings and emotions.

Take it further:

Which of our other senses can produce feelings, atmospheres and emotions? For example, think of sights that you might see that would make you feel: sad/happy and excited/relaxed or sleepy.

As One Door Closes

Key ideas:

There's a saying: 'As one door closes another one opens ...'

Life is often like that. We sometimes see something that we think is just right for us, and then feel thoroughly dejected that we can't have it for some reason. We just can't understand it at all, it seemed so right. But then other opportunities arise, and often we're glad we didn't get the first option after all. And then we wonder if there was a reason why things turned out as they did.

Sam found himself in a long corridor. Along each side there were doors of every colour, and some had windows that you could look through. Other people were with him – some he knew, some he didn't. Several of them were trying the doors – and sometimes they opened and then they would go into that room.

'Which door shall I choose?' he thought.

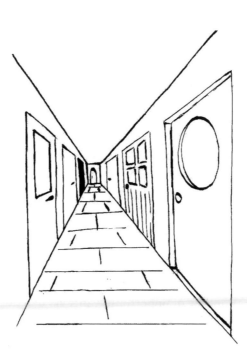

He looked through the window of a yellow door. The room was empty and lonely looking. It had very little furniture and no windows. 'No,' thought Sam, 'I don't like the look of that room.'

He walked a bit further along the corridor looking into other rooms until he reached a bright blue door with an oval window. Looking through the window Sam saw a fantastic room with bright walls, tables full of rich food and attractive people talking to each other and smiling.

'Wow!' he said. 'That's the place for me!' He turned the handle and pushed the door.

But the door wouldn't open. He paused. 'Come on,' he said to himself, 'Open.' But the door stayed firmly shut. 'Why won't it open?' he cried in frustration. 'I'm meant to be in that room.'

'Excuse me,' said a voice behind him.

A boy pushed past. He turned the handle of the door and, to Sam's amazement, the door opened straightaway. The boy looked at Sam and grinned. 'Bye,' he said and closed the door in Sam's face.

'That's just not fair!' shouted Sam, 'I should be in there, not you.' He tried to open the door again, but no matter how hard he pushed it just wouldn't open. He slumped onto the floor in despair. 'I'm never going to get in,' he said. 'I'm going to be stuck out here on my own forever.'

And then across the corridor, further along, he saw another blue door. It wasn't quite the same shade as the one he'd been trying – it was a lighter shade of blue, but it was worth a look. He peered through the window in the light blue door. The room wasn't quite as bright as the first room, but the colours of the walls were warmer. 'That room doesn't look bad,' he thought.

Hoping against hope, he tried turning the handle. There was a soft click and as he pushed the door gently it swung open. Into the room he went, and the more he looked around, the more he liked this place. It just felt – comfortable – the right place for him.

There were other people there too. They were happy and friendly and really pleased to be there. 'Come on in,' they said, 'we'll show you around.' At the far side of the room was another window and as Sam passed it he found that he was looking into the room with the dark blue door. The people in that room were still smiling, but none of them seemed happy. And at the far side of the room was the boy who had pushed past him – sitting on a stool by himself and looking sad.

To do:

- Talk about the phrases: 'Window of opportunity' and 'As one door closes another opens'. These are often used as metaphors for things that happen to us in our lives.

- You could ask the children to describe or draw their perfect place, or their hopes for where they might be. It could be drawn as a room or series of rooms with doors and windows.

- Should 'doors' always open for us? Do we always get the things we want?

- Ask the children to think of their own life experiences. Has there been an instance when there was something they really wanted to do, when everything seemed so right, but for some reason the opportunity wasn't realised?

Take it further:

Sometimes people say: 'Looking back I can understand why that happened. It was meant to be.' Discuss the idea of 'destiny' – and that some religions believe there is a plan for our lives, which is already mapped out for us. Talk about the idea of a plan for our lives.

A Story of Circles

Key ideas:

The folly of trying to control what is beyond us. The notion that the world will take care of itself. The story also uses the important metaphor of the properties of water to explore what is mysterious in our lives.

Long ago there was a warrior chief called Tso Chan, whose power and ambition were great but whose arrogance was greater still. One day he decided to conquer new lands and so called for his mightiest general, whose name was Silent Blade.

'The time has come when I must expand my nation,' Tso Chan said. 'Look there in the valley. The land is green and fertile. The people are soft. Conquest will be easy. Assemble my warriors!'

By noon 500 armed men were marching down from the north. They came softly, so all that could be heard was the musical clink and tinkling of metal on metal. Well before dusk Tso Chan caught sight of the first village in the valley. It was a beautiful place; a cluster of huts made from sticks and mud-brick, roofed with a thatch of rice stems. A large clearing in the middle formed a space where meetings took place, although now only children could be seen playing there.

One of them, a little girl named Su Mai, noticed the afternoon sun sparkling on the weapons of the approaching soldiers. She stared at this unusual sight for some moments, then hurried away to tell the grown-ups. By the time Tso Chan led his army into the clearing, the villagers had assembled there to greet them.

Tso Chan, with his chest puffed out and a huge sword clasped in his hands, looked about himself sneeringly. 'I am the great Tso Chan, king of the mountain peoples! I have come to conquer this puny land. Where is your chief, that he may bow down before me?'

There was a rustling among the villagers and an old man stepped forward. This ancient fellow had wispy white hair and a beard as fine as cobweb. He was stooped with age, and needed to walk with a stick made from river willow wood. When Tso Chan caught sight of him he laughed aloud.

'Surely you are not the ruler of these rice-growers!'

'My name,' replied the old one, 'is San Kuo Yen. And you are quite right, mighty Tso Chan. I do not rule these people. We are all ruled equally by the seasons.'

Tso Chan found himself irritated by this answer, which sounded rather too clever for him to understand. 'Bow down before me, old man, for I am your conqueror!' Tso Chan waved his sword around menacingly.

'Alas, great king, the years have made me bow down as far as I am able. And while you may indeed conquer this village, time itself conquers all in the end.'

Again the old man seemed to have given a reply that Tso Chan was unable to argue against. But it annoyed him nevertheless, so he decided to show these simple villagers something of his wisdom and his might. 'Now listen to me, old man; listen to me all of you!' Tso Chan took his sword and scratched a circle in the dust. 'That is what you people understand…' Then Tso Chan scraped a much larger circle around the first. 'And that is what I understand – so beware!'

He stood back and leaned on his sword, his chest puffed out even further. The villagers muttered amongst themselves, then looked to San Kuo Yen to reply. The old man nodded presently and stroked his beard.

'Yes, yes, you are quite correct, oh powerful Tso Chan. There is much I do not know…' And as everyone watched, he used his crooked willow stick to draw a much, much larger circle around the other two. 'But this is what neither of us understands, great leader, so we should *all* beware…'

San Kuo Yen's answer enraged Tso Chan because it stung his pride. And yet, once again, he found it impossible to disagree with what the old man said.

'That may be so, peasant! But I am Tso Chan the conqueror! You have taught me something, I admit. And it is this… I had thought to make only this valley part of my kingdom. But now I will go further, out into the wider world. I will find the boundaries of that outer circle, and learn everything there is to be learned. Then I will return in triumph and you will at last recognise my greatness.'

San Kuo Yen lifted his head up to look into Tso Chan's fiery eyes. 'You are doing something I would never dare to do,' the old man admitted. 'I hope you have an interesting search.'

Tso Chan gazed upon the crippled wise man for a moment longer then raised his sword and beckoned for Silent Blade and all his soldiers to follow. The army marched away into the distance and the villagers watched them go, before returning to their work.

But many of the children stared after the dwindling warriors with concern in their eyes. The little girl, Su Mai, tugged gently on the sleeve of San Kuo Yen's cotton tunic. 'What will happen when Tso Chan *does* learn all that is to be learned; when he has found the edge of that outer circle? He will come back, won't he, and take our animals and crops?'

'Well,' said San Kuo Yen, 'there is something that Tso Chan did not realise and that I, being a forgetful old fool, did not think to explain. We drew our circles in dust, but really they should have been drawn on water.'

'How is that possible?' asked Su Mai.

'Walk with me to the lake,' San Kuo Yen said to her and the other children. 'And I will show you.'

They wandered over to the lake, right to the shore between clumps of tall reeds. San Kuo Yen asked Su Mai to pass him a pebble off the ground. 'Here are the things the mighty Tso Chan wanted to learn, written on water,' San Kuo Yen said, pitching the pebble high into the air. It splashed down into the lake, sending ripples circling away from the point where it had landed. The children watched the outer circle growing, growing, growing, until finally it faded completely away.

Then, with smiles on their faces, they bowed to San Kuo Yen in thanks and returned with lighter hearts to their play.

To do:

■ Discussion points can include:

◆ Does trying to force and control people ever lead to happiness?

◆ Do we need to go outside our ordinary life to find enlightenment (of whatever kind)?

■ How else can the metaphor of water help us to develop our spiritual side? (Note: Water is the central image of the philosophical tradition of Taoism. See 'Wu Wei' on pages 42–43).

Spirituality is an acceptance that we have another dimension in addition to our physical, mental and social wellbeing.

I accept that there is a force or power at play in us and in the world that cannot fully be understood. The name Catholics give it is the Holy Spirit. It can be found in our hearts and soul ... if you look hard enough!

I have found a sense of liberation in the realisation that spirituality cannot be fully understood or explained. But I know it's there ...

I know the wind is there because I can feel it and see its effects.

Michael Barry

Activities

The Endless Story

Key ideas:

Examining the deep-rooted desire to 'narratise'; to create stories as a way of explaining what happens in life.

A good story is often called 'a real page turner', where the reader is swept along with the excitements of the plot as the hero battles against apparently insurmountable odds until at last the villain is defeated, loose ends are tied up and the problem is resolved.

But notice that final word, which means in fact 're-solved' or solved again. Nothing is settled finally and forever. There is no grand and ultimate happy ending – or sad ending come to that. Because there will always be evil, there will always be the need for good. In this sense the white knight and the dragon are in eternal conflict – or perhaps 'creative tension' would be a better way of thinking about it.

This endless story, reflected the world over in countless myths, legends and hero tales, fits what has been called the basic template of narrative, as in the figure below.

This is the basic shape of a narrative:

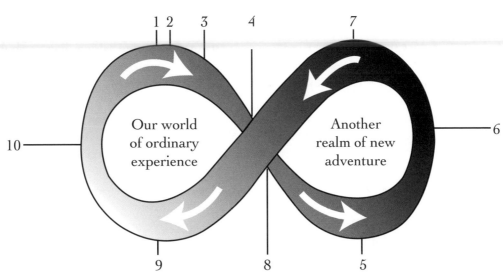

The ten significant points are:

1. The hero's call to action

2. Heeding the call

3. The first descent into danger

4. The threshold to new experience

5. Point of lowest ebb and giving up hope

6. The time of greatest ordeal

7. Point of false optimism

8. Recrossing the threshold

9. A twist in the tale (for example a shock or surprise)

10. Hero's return home and a restoring of balance and harmony

The basic elements or 'building blocks' of a narrative are:

Hero, Villain, Problem, Journey, Partner, Help, Power (gained through Knowledge), Object.

Typically a story features the hero figure in his/her ordinary life. Then comes the 'call to adventure'. Following this the hero faces a number of challenges, crises and ordeals before defeating the villain and restoring order and balance to life. Although the adventure is perhaps new to any particular hero, others have walked this path since our species arose, and will continue to re-solve life's difficulties until we come to our ending. Is it a coincidence that this shape – ∞ – is also the mathematical symbol for infinity?

To do:

■ You can introduce the idea of the narrative template to children by asking them to consider how their own favourite stories fit that pattern. Ask them also to identify the fundamental elements of hero, villain and so on.

■ In looking at their own stories, have children consider how the narrative could be made more powerful by superimposing it on the template (given that they haven't done this already).

■ Using the template and building blocks write your own adventure story.

■ Look at real examples of heroism. What is the larger narrative or context within which these acts of courage, altruism, compassion and so on occur?

Take it further:

Help children to 'transfer the skill' of knowing how the template works to address life's problems – imaginary or real situations, as appropriate. What heroic qualities are needed to resolve them?

One class made a board game by using the ∞ shape, dividing it up into a number of squares and thinking of challenges and crises that faced the hero on his/her journey.

Links:

Central narrative elements of the endless story template are (in addition to hero and villain): a journey, partner, help, knowledge and power, a significant object. To find out more about these see Vladimir Propp's *Morphology of the Folktale* and Steve Bowkett's *StoryMaker Catch Pack*.

Spirituality is an atmosphere around an individual who is connected to the wider universe. People who remember and partake in equinox and solstice know there is something that those events trigger in their minds, heart and ultimately soul. Ancient burial sites and stone circles have an atmosphere about them that evokes feelings from within. Spirituality fulfils an inner desire within me that I search for in various ways, it is a journey to connect to a past consciousness.

Charlie Folorunsho

Once Upon a Time There Was a Giant

Once upon a time there was a giant and the giant scared the little boy. And then the boy get a sword and then the boy get a bow and arrow and the boy get a dragon. Now the giant was scared.

Story by Darnell, aged 3

Illustration by Maleek, aged 5

Spirituality is the connection between what is deep down inside you and what is way out there beyond you. It has absolutely nothing to do with what is in between.

Ian Gilbert

Story Mapping

Key idea:

To explore the creation of meaning.

To do:

- On a piece of paper draw a curvy line from one side of the paper to the other. Then invite pupils to suggest random natural phenomena, characters, objects and environments using the Story Mapping Planning Sheet from the CD.

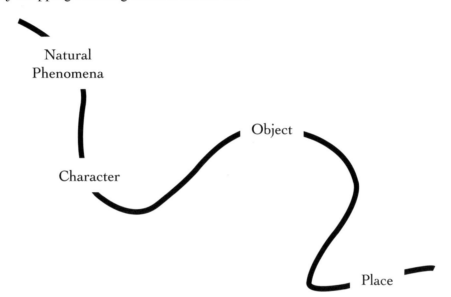

Natural
Phenomena

Character

Object

Place

- Create interesting groupings of these as demonstrated below.

    Example 1:

Natural phenomenon:	Snow
Character:	Prince
Object:	An empty birdcage
Place:	A lake

    Example 2:

Natural phenomenon:	Volcano
Character:	Old woman
Object:	An oil lamp
Place:	Cave

■ Once you have a range of possible examples divide them between your class. Invite pupils to work together in twos or threes using all three ingredients to write a creation myth explaining the natural phenomenon in their example. For example:

The Day the Sun Refused to Set

Natural phenomenon:	Sunset
Character:	Girl
Object:	A mirror
Place:	The desert

Once a long, long time ago, before time as we knew it began, the people of the Earth used to weep and wail each night when the sun disappeared fearing that it may never return.

And so the sun, on hearing this, decided to sit in the sky and refuse to set.

'I am so radiant and beautiful and glorious and everyone loves me so much that I will stay in the sky forever and make the world happy,' thought the sun.

And for a while everyone was happy. People loved the warmth of the sun and the light it gave them. But after a while the lakes and oceans began to dry up, the plants began to wilt and a famine came into the land.

As the world dried up, the earth turned to sand and everywhere began to resemble a desert. People were thirsty but had no water to drink. But the sun didn't notice and continued to sit in the heavens thinking that the people of the world thought it beautiful.

Now one of the people affected by the sun at this time was a young girl who lived on the edge of the fastest growing desert in the world. At night she covered her head with blankets in the hope that she might make it dark enough to get some sleep, but the sun was too hot and the blankets made her hotter so she found it hard to rest.

One day, thirsty and tired, the girl decided she had had enough. She walked out into the desert and called up to the sun in her loudest voice.

'You need to stop shining all the time. It's too hot down here. You're killing all the plants,' she shouted loudly and clearly, and amazingly the sun heard.

'But I thought everyone loved me,' replied the sun. 'People are always so happy when I am around.'

'But we also need the moon, we need the night to rest and we also need rain to water the land,' called the girl. But the sun was still confused.

'I thought I was making everyone happy. It is such fun to shine all the time and be beautiful and bright.'

'But you're too bright, you're hurting the world!' the girl shouted. And then reaching into her bag she took out a mirror and placed it in the direct line of the sun so it could see itself reflected.

'Ow! What's that, you're blinding me,' called the sun.

'It's you,' replied the girl and suddenly the sun understood. It was definitely beautiful and definitely brilliant, but it was also hot and blinding when it shone too brightly or for too long.

'You need to give the world a rest each evening,' called the girl, 'but please leave us a sign as you go to make sure we know you are coming back as we do miss you when you are gone.'

And the sun smiled and nodded at the girl and a pact was made between them.

From then onwards the sun set at the end of each day, and as it moved away from the sky it made sure it left behind it a palette of beautiful colours, keeping its promise to the girl and reminding the people of Earth that it would definitely return.

God is internal not external, implicit not explicit, personal not universal.

Jules

Quiet Moments

Key ideas:

Enjoying the peace that may be found in quietness. Creating opportunities for reflective thinking or simple appreciation.

I don't think I've ever read or been told that spiritual insights can't be gained in a busy, noisy environment. Indeed to be amongst a large crowd at some inspiring event – the Olympics, a rock concert, a carnival, a religious congregation – could not fail to be uplifting. The very idea of a crowd united for some common purpose gives a hint of that essentially indescribable experience of being connected to *everything* that exists. Also we can lose ourselves within large groups, in the sense that we become completely absorbed in the situation or event, having lost if only briefly our self-consciousness and sense of being separate.

But quietness too is valuable since it allows the world to pass by without us having to be involved. Moments of tranquillity invite reflectiveness – a pause for thought if you like. Such occasions, combined with deliberate and enjoyable activity, create an intimacy of experience and allow us to notice and appreciate its smallest of details. Here are a few ideas that you might try out or at least suggest to the children.

To do:

■ Noticing the breath. Sitting quietly, just be aware of your own breathing. Realise how easily breathing happens, how the air flows in and out of the body all by itself. Feeling more and more settled is just as effortless. Focus your awareness on the sensation of the cool air streaming in through your nose (or mouth). This is an ancient practice and the precursor to meditation – two good books on this are Barry Long's *Meditation* and Naomi Ozaniec's *101 Essential Tips: Everyday Meditation.*

■ Hearing without listening, seeing without looking. Just put yourself in a pleasing environment, close your eyes and simply hear the many different sounds that come to your ears all by themselves. There's no need to count, identify or otherwise think about them. Just hear for its own sake. Opening your eyes, simply appreciate the view. Just be aware of shapes and colours and movement. No need to do anything else.

Take it further:

■ Under the heavens. For me there is nothing more awe inspiring than sitting out on a clear night watching the stars. This experience is especially powerful if you are in the country where there is less noise and light pollution. It takes around twenty minutes for your eyes to become 'dark adapted', after which time the degree of faint detail you can see is amazing.

■ Miniature Zen gardens. Do an Internet search to pick up some quick ideas. You'll need a small tray or box, sand or fine gravel, stones, shells, leaves, glass beads and so on, and a fork or tiny rake. Enjoy the simple act of arranging a small number of these objects on a bed of gravel or sand. Use the rake to create curving lines and swirls. Why bother? For the simple act of creation. Only later might you want to think about what the arrangement of objects and patterns could mean to you.

Looking from Another Angle

Many of us as children loved looking up at the clouds and imagining a wealth of stories arising from each of them. Look at the picture above – what do you see? A super bunny launching off into space?

But what happens if we view the cloud from a different angle? Perhaps you now see a wineglass shattering, or a sea anemone growing up from the ocean floor?

Changing the viewpoint means we see something from an entirely different perspective. Suddenly what we thought we saw is not necessarily what we now see when we look at it in a different way.

Near the top right hand side of the photo perhaps you can see a ballet dancer twirling onto the scene in her flowing dress. She certainly was not there when we look at the image above.

A fresh viewpoint and the image changes again. Perhaps this third image is of a whale diving down to the bottom of the sea with its hungry mouth open.

The dancing ballerina from the previous view has changed into a small goldfish which hasn't yet realised that he is swimming straight into the jaws of danger.

The same picture moved around and viewed from different angles tells a very different story.

As for the final image, perhaps this time you can see a big giant's face with a laughing mouth and a pig-style nose filling the sky as he stares down at the people below.

To do:

Belinda Hopkins from Transforming Conflict invented an exercise where you place a piece of material on the floor and ask the group to stand around it in a circle.

Each member of the group says what they can see in much the same way as looking at the clouds and describing the pictures. Then when everyone has described their side of the story they move in a circle around the cloth so that everyone is standing in a different place.

Again the group takes it in turns to say what they can see. The fact that everyone can see something totally different when they move to a different place is hugely apparent. By changing the angle we look at something from the story we see changes. Transforming Conflict use this as a metaphor in their Restorative Approaches – reminding us that the side that we have seen is not always the full picture.

This is equally relevant in developing spiritual intelligence. We can't always see the full picture. Sometimes we need to move around a bit, change our position and look from a fresh angle.

■ Use the worksheet to write down what you think spirituality is.

■ Use the 'Looking from Another Angle' worksheet to write down what you can see.

Moral Obligation

Key idea:

To explore morals and obligations.

To do:

■ Do you have a moral obligation to help in the following situations or not? Place the list below into the following table.

Strong Moral Obligation	Weak Moral Obligation	No Moral Obligation

◆ Someone you don't know needs a kidney to survive and yours is a direct match. How obligated are you to give them your kidney?

◆ What if the person who needed your kidney was a relative?

◆ A person from your school is guilty of a crime against another child. You know they did it, but how morally obligated are you to report them to a teacher?

◆ What if the person who was hurt is your best friend?

◆ On the way home from school you pass a homeless person begging on the street. They ask you for money. You have £3 in change in your pocket. What is your moral obligation to them?

◆ You have to choose between giving ten people in your school an injection that will protect them from contracting a serious illness, or you can protect 100 people in Africa from the disease. You cannot do both. What is your moral obligation to the people in your school? Should you protect them from harm?

◆ What is your moral obligation to the 100 people in Africa? Are you obliged to protect them from harm?

◆ You spill paint on the teacher's chair by accident and don't tell anyone. She doesn't realise and sits down on it. At the end of the day she walks out of the classroom and the back of her dress is covered in paint. She has told the class she is going somewhere special that evening. How morally obligated are you to tell her about the paint?

Harmony and Discord

Key ideas:

When musical notes are played together they can create responses and feelings. Some note combinations are pleasing on the ear, others aren't and sometimes it is a matter of personal taste. Some note combinations evoke moods and feelings – major chords evoke positive and happy feelings whilst minor chords seem sad. When people come together there can be harmony or disharmony in a similar sense.

Have you ever played an old piano? Maybe you're one of those 'Chopsticks' people that as soon as you're in a room with an old piano, start playing with your two index fingers.

Or maybe you don't know where to start.

Middle C is a good place to start – that's the white one above the keyhole with two black keys to the right of it that look like gaps in your teeth.

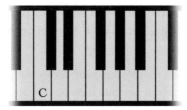

First play the middle C. Then going to your right where the notes get higher, you miss out a white note and play the next white one (that's an E because it goes up like the alphabet). Then you miss another one and play the next: that's G.

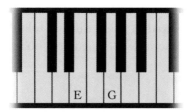

Now with your thumb on middle C play all three notes together. Play it again and listen to the sound – is it a happy sound or sad sound? Now play middle C with your middle finger, E with your little finger and the white key two down from middle C (which is an A) with your thumb. Play the chord a few times – is it a happy sound or sad sound?

Happy sounding chords are usually major (the one we played was called C major because C was at the bottom). Sad sounding chords are often from a minor key. The one we played starting on A is called A minor – you may know all about major and minor scales if you're learning to play an instrument. Play the two chords a few times, one then the other, and change your expression as you do so.

When musical notes are played together they form chords. When it sounds nice we say they are in harmony with each other. When it doesn't sound nice we call it a discord. We also use the words harmony and discord to describe how people get on with each other – or not!

To do:

■ Think about people that you are in harmony with. Why do you think this is – that is, what makes you get on with them? Is it shared interests, similarities in personality or a similar approach to life?

■ Think of someone with whom you produce discord – perhaps someone you don't get on with very well. Why do you think this is?

■ How could you turn this discord into harmony – do some of the notes in your personality need to change?

Take it further:

Are you in harmony with yourself? Do other people generally see you as a major key or minor key person – or a discordant one?

The World Is Wiggly but Not Wobbly

Key ideas:

The deepest meanings in life may go beyond our ability to analyse or even express them. Being alive in the world means being part of continual 'flow' and change. Everything moves and interacts in an infinite number of ways. To look at some 'thing' is like seeing one frame of a movie. Life is about living through the whole movie.

I have referred to the philosopher Alan Watts (who died in 1973) a number of times in my contribution to this book. His great achievement was to make the ideas behind the philosophy of Taoism and Zen Buddhism accessible to ordinary people, and to link those ideas to the ordinary lives that we lead. He clarified without becoming simplistic, he enthused without gushing, he influenced without trying to coerce. For me Watts remains one of the most inspirational voices in the whole field of spiritual intelligence.

One of his insights is to insist that the world is 'wiggly'. By this he means that nothing is static; everything is in motion and flow. This is easy to appreciate when we look at a river or flames or a time-lapse film of plants growing and flowering. But Watts goes beyond this and points out, for instance, that the wiggliness of a door is just as real. Not only are its atoms in constant motion, but what we perceive as a door is a kind of snapshot in the movie of a seed on its journey to returning to the soil – seed, sapling, tree, planks, door, discarded and rotting, nourishing more seeds.

In explaining this elegant notion Watts asks us to consider an ocean wave as it surges in and laps up on the shore. What we think we see is a wave moving closer, though actually what's happening is that energy not water moves across the ocean's surface: the water molecules themselves simply travel in small circles as the energy passes through. In this sense what we observe is not 'a wave' but the ocean 'waving'. We touch on this idea in 'Going Yourself' (see page 94): I am not 'my self', I am 'selving'. I don't see apples on the tree, I see the tree 'appling'.

41

To do:

One application (apple-ication?) of this idea is to encourage children to see everyday objects as 'wiggling' – moving like the energy in the ocean as it gives rise to what seem to be discrete things. In one class children made flicker-books to illustrate the point. One boy drew simple pictures of baby–child–youth–man–old man–skeleton. Another child traced the wave or wiggle of an apple seed as it 'appled' into a tree, fell back eventually into the earth and gave rise to further life. Use the worksheet with the children so they can see their objects wiggle.

Take it further:

Help children to explore the question, 'Who am I?' This usually gives rise to long lists or extensive mindmaps of things *about* individuals. These contribute to our sense of self and who we suppose we are, but in the end amount to no more than a piece of seaweed carried along on a wave.

Related to these ideas is the old Zen advice: In walking, just walk. In sitting, just sit. Above all, don't wobble (Yun-Men 862–949 CE). This tells us that since we are all selving anyway (and can't do anything else) we might as well do it, as they say 'with gusto'.

Wu Wei (Whooee!) – Going Along for the Ride

Key ideas:

Looking at the notion that 'life happens anyway' and that trying to force things to happen, and to control, does not lead to a heightening of spiritual awareness.

Imagine listening to some pleasant music or gazing at a landscape on a sunny day. These are things that are easy to do. We don't try to do them – they are not 'activities' in that sense, but neither are we passive during the experience. The music flows easily through us, we sit and absorb the beautiful landscape without effort. We might also consider the idea that while the listening or the gazing are going on, we and the sounds and the scene are all part and parcel of the same thing. It makes no sense to try to separate the music from the listener or the landscape from the observer. The whole occurrence simply unfolds with us as an integral part of it.

Reflecting on this further we can appreciate that the natural world operates entirely in accordance with this idea of 'not trying' or not forcing. There is a seamless unfolding of events in nature, an effortless integration of all that happens. I was out for the day recently with a friend and at one point he glanced at the sky and said, 'Look it's trying to rain.' It was only a throwaway comment but it got me thinking. Of course the sky and clouds were not trying to rain at all. The rain would happen or not depending on all kinds of interrelated factors. Soon afterwards it did rain, all by itself, effortlessly.

These are not frivolous ideas, though they are subtle. Western culture makes use of many metaphors that emphasise struggle, conflict and dominance. In education, for instance, we talk of children keeping up or slipping back as we cover ground. There are aims and targets and objectives – all military metaphors before they were educational ones. And when we have understood some field of knowledge to a high degree we are masters of it.

I am certainly not arguing against hard work: the writer Ian Fleming said that effort is desirable for its own sake and that those who succeed through their own endeavours are heroes. Similarly when John F. Kennedy committed the United States to putting a man on the moon by 1970 he told his audience at Rice University that this would be attempted 'not because it is easy, but because it is hard'. (See http://www.historyplace.com/speeches/jfk-space.htm for the entire speech.)

However, I think that while trying is appropriate and effective in some circumstances, *not* forcing, *not* struggling works better in others. As the writer Arthur C. Clarke advises, 'cooperate with the inevitable'. The Chinese philosophy of Taoism contains a similar concept known as *wu wei*, which means not forcing or not obstructing; not getting in your own way, going with the grain. This also implies a lack of self-consciousness. If I hear a funny joke I laugh. I don't try to force a laugh. And when I laugh spontaneously I am not being self-conscious about it; I'm not thinking about my laughter or analysing it.

To do:

These ideas have many implications in developing spiritual intelligence generally and in helping children to function practically day by day. Here's how you might start:

- Explain that some things happen automatically, 'all by themselves'. Have children think of examples from nature. In fact the elegant concept of ecology is essentially what *wu wei* is about.

- Point out that knowing when to act and when to leave things alone often gets the best results. A good gardener will tend the plants but doesn't try to make them grow (although discussing the concept of force growing might prove interesting here). Make a list of other instances on the worksheet.

- Explore with the class the powerful metaphor of flowing water. If this was applied to the way we live, how might things be different?

Truth or Lie

Key idea:

To explore the meaning of the word truth. What is true and what is a lie?

To do:

■ Standing or sitting in a circle take it in turns to introduce yourself to the group, saying your name and one thing that is true about your life. It could be as simple as 'I have an older sister', or you might choose to be more revealing about something: 'I am frightened of spiders'. In this part of the exercise you can say anything about yourself but it has to be true.

■ Once everyone has had a turn go round the circle again but this time everyone has to say something that is not true. It could be something totally fictitious, 'I can fly by flapping my arms in the air', or something that is plausible but not actually true, 'I have a younger brother'.

■ Once everyone has had a turn, invite the group to discuss the exercise. Did they enjoy making up something about themselves? Was it fun to pretend something was true that wasn't?

■ Next ask the group if they think they were lying when they told everyone the thing that was not true.

■ Try to come up with a definition for lying that you can all agree with as a group.

■ Next think about the following scenarios and place them in a Venn diagram. Are the examples below definitely truth, lie or do they fit somewhere in the grey area in the middle?

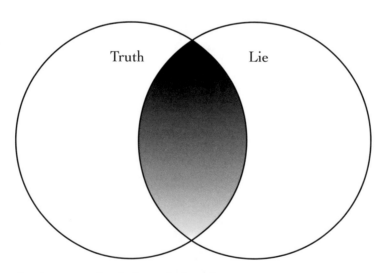

◆ Your mum has just come back from the hairdresser. You think her hair looks awful and the new colour doesn't suit her at all. She asks for your opinion and you tell her it looks lovely. Are you lying if you are protecting someone's feelings?

◆ You have a test the next day at school that you haven't revised for, and you hardly sleep that night for worrying about it. In the morning you tell your mum that you are not well and manage to get the day off school. Are you lying if you are really feeling tired from not sleeping?

◆ Your teacher tells off your best friend for leaving the art area in a mess. You know it wasn't him and you are worried because he has got into a lot of trouble recently and you want to save him from more. You put your hand up and tell the teacher that it was you who left the art tables in a mess. Are you lying when you are helping out a friend?

◆ You are at a friend's house with several of your friends. They have a large cake on the table and you end up eating rather more than your share of it. Your friend's mum asks who ate the last slice and although it was you, you don't say anything. Are you lying when you don't say anything?

◆ Are there any other scenarios you can think of that explore situations of truth or lie? Is it ever okay to tell a lie? Why do people lie?

Yes, but Where's the Proof?

Key ideas:

Exploring the idea that spiritual awareness is not something that can be found through looking for solid proof, or even by logical reasoning. Looking at the conflict that exists between science and religion – and investigating where we stand in this great debate.

In recent years the voice of the 'evangelical atheist' has re-entered the public arena with the appearance of books such as Richard Dawkins's *The God Delusion*, in which he appears to conclude that God probably doesn't exist but we don't know for sure. Ultra sceptics like Professor Dawkins look through the window and see a purposeless world created entirely by random chance and the blind force of evolution. Others such as the poet and Anglican priest R. S. Thomas see the handiwork of God manifest as though it were a painting, always complete but never finished (see 'The View from the Window' in his *Selected Poems, 1946–1948*).

What I think is most important in children's spiritual development is for them to explore the issue and make up their own minds. Philosophical discussion can help, although one could argue that faith and spiritual enlightenment are essentially not to do with the intellect or rational thought at all.

To do:

A useful technique for helping children to 'get their thoughts in order' is to have them write down their ideas, opinions and points of argument on scraps of paper. Create several sets of scraps, one for each working group, then invite the groups to separate out the scraps into two piles – points for the existence of a deity and points against. Further organise each pile in order of the relevance or persuasive power of each point. This will generate a great deal of lively discussion. Individual scraps can be placed in the centre of a large blank sheet and mindmaps created around them as further ideas are generated. Below (see figure) are a number of points that you can use to kick-start the children's debate on the issue.

Science has shown that the universe could have arisen from nothing, so God isn't necessary.	Humans couldn't have developed just by chance – there are just too many coincidences involved.	How come so many people believe in one God or another if He or She or It doesn't exist? Why do we have religious faiths at all?
Religion and God are just ideas to help us feel comfortable and safe, that there is some kind of point to our lives.	If God is so wise and loving, why is there pain and suffering in the world? Because there is, and evil too, surely God can't exist.	Without evil we would not know how to be good. Without suffering there could be no compassion. The world is set up like this so we have a choice.
Just because millions of people believe in God doesn't make them right. People used to believe the Earth was flat.	Lots of people believe in God just because their parents or their society tells them to.	There's no scientific evidence that God exists
Science can't tell us everything. God is beyond science.	If God made the universe, who made God?	The living world works so beautifully – so it must have been designed.

Link:

Stephen Law's books *The Philosophy Files 1* and *2* contain useful advice on how children can 'do philosophy' as well as a fascinating exploration of 'does God exist?'

Discovering Self

Stories

The Well

Key idea:

Sometimes having an answer is not as important as finding the right question.

No one could recall who first built the well. It was as if it had always been there. There were no records of names and dates that could point to the moment in time when a voice said 'here is the place'. The well had served the village for centuries and it was expected and assumed that it would continue to do so for years to come. Whilst the well provided water for all the basic needs of everyone in the village (washing, cooking, cleaning and, of course, drinking) it held other secrets that few had ever discovered.

Shijo was used to fetching and carrying water from the well to home. This was the task of most of the children of the village. It happened twice a day, every day, and sometimes during the day should either thirst or chores require an extra journey. Shijo was the only child, and therefore had many chores and tasks to complete. He seldom complained. His father had died when Shijo was only 7 and from that moment he had worked tirelessly to support his mother in any way he could. In order to earn money his mother washed other people's laundry and this meant that Shijo would have to carry more water more often than any of the other children in the village. Years of fetching and carrying had made Shijo fit and strong. Several times during the day he could be seen carrying the two large traditional wooden pails balanced across his shoulders on a pole that made him look, from a distance, like a set of walking scales.

It was one of these times when, after a particularly busy day cleaning, that water was needed and Shijo was sent out to fetch two more buckets.

The walk to the well took fifteen minutes, the walk back took thirty. Carrying water took not only strength but care. Rushing back could mean spilling the contents and this meant a return journey to the well.

Arriving at the well Shijo saw an old man struggling to pull his bucket that was full of water to the top of the well. Shijo asked the man if he would like some help. The old man nodded vigorously and Shijo moved in front of the man and began to pull. The weight of the water was far heavier than Shijo had ever experienced.

'His bucket must be made of lead,' he thought.

Finally, after much hard work the bucket was pulled to the top of the well and lowered safely onto the floor.

'Thank you,' the old man said. He then put his hand into the bucket and pulled out a gold tube. At one end of the tube was a stopper in the shape of a circle with a small but definite dot in the middle. The old man began to turn the stopper and it slowly unscrewed and finally came free revealing a hollow tube out of which the old man pulled a rolled up sheet of paper known in those ancient times as parchment.

The old man read the words on the parchment, nodded slowly in agreement and placed the parchment back in the tube and sealed it up. Turning to Shijo he said: 'It was a kind thing that you did, more helpful than you know. Now, let me tell you something of great importance. This is a magic well and this is a magic container. Inside is a piece of enchanted paper and a quill that will always be inked but only when used to write a question on this parchment. I have been coming to this well for years in search of answers to problems that I have encountered on my journey through life. This is the last time I will visit the well and therefore the last time that I will need this container. I would like you to have it.'

Shijo was about to politely refuse the old man's kindness as he could see the immense value of the golden container, but the old man raised his hand to stop him speaking.

'I know that you might think this is too valuable a gift. But it is on loan. You could sell it but that would be to deny the real value of this gift. The magic works like this. Write your question on this parchment and place it into the container and lower it down the well. Each time you ask a question the further down the well you have to lower the bucket. This means that at some point you will ask a question that will require you to lower the bucket to a depth where you can barely manage to pull it to the surface. Today was that day for me. Whoever comes and offers help will be the person you have been waiting for. Read your final message and give the golden cylinder to this stranger as I am giving it to you. The knowledge and wisdom that you can discover if you ask the right questions will be worth more than gold and benefit more people than just you.'

With that the old man handed the cylinder to Shijo and picked up his single bucket and walked away.

For a short while Shijo did not know what to do. Was the old man mad? Should he just sell the cylinder or melt it down. He decided to test the truth of the old man's words and unscrewed the cylinder. Inside were the parchment and the magic quill.

Shijo took out the paper as the old man had advised him. It was blank and he touched the tip of the quill and began to write. To his great surprise, despite the fact there was no ink on the quill, his words appeared on the page. He wrote a question that had been in his mind for a long time. A question – that if he knew the answer – would make him understand more about what he was to do with his life and where he should put his efforts.

He sealed the cylinder with the paper inside and lowered the bucket down. He let it go a little while deeper than he normally did and noticed that, although manageable, the bucket was heavier than normal and he had to put more effort into raising it to the surface.

As soon as the bucket was safely on the ground Shijo opened the cylinder and took out the paper. His hands were shaking as he unravelled the paper. His question was there and so was an answer, written in the most beautiful and elaborate handwriting. The answer was 'in time, with constant effort and an open heart, you will'. Shijo smiled contentedly as the words faded and the page returned to its blank state.

Shijo put the paper alongside the quill back into the cylinder and sealed it. He then filled up the second bucket (which seemed much lighter that the first) and returned home to his mother.

Over the coming years Shijo would return to the well and pose a question. During his time in the village Shijo became a much respected, wealthy and wise man who assisted the people of the town in many ways. His major contribution was to build a school, which is still there to this day.

Years passed. When Shijo was much older he took a single bucket to the well and wrote down a question on the parchment: 'Is my work here complete?' He sealed the cylinder and lowered the bucket so far down that he had nearly no rope to hold onto. However, the weight was too great and Shijo was too old and weak and could not lift it.

'Can I help?' a voice asked. Shijo turned to see a young woman standing by him. He nodded furiously not wishing to waste an ounce of energy.

The girl though small was very strong and determined and soon the bucket was on the floor. Shijo took out the cylinder and read the message. He smiled and nodded in agreement.

Turning to the girl Shijo gave the cylinder to her as the old man had given it to him all those years before. He explained the value of the gift as it had been explained to him. He then lifted his bucket full to the brim with water and for the last time carried it back to his house.

The girl stood for a while pondering on what had just happened. She then opened the cylinder and wrote a question that was to change her life forever.

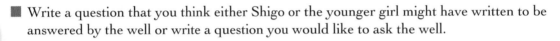

To do:

Explore the questions that were asked in the story by asking the children:

■ What was the question that Shijo asked at the beginning?

■ What was the question that the girl wrote that was going to change her life forever?

■ If they had a magic parchment what would they ask and how could this help them in life?

■ Write a question that you think either Shigo or the younger girl might have written to be answered by the well or write a question you would like to ask the well.

Take it further:

Turn this into a Q&A game. Each child writes one sentence of practical advice on a small piece of paper. Examples might be: ask for help from someone you trust; share your thoughts with a friend; think twice before you do anything; learn something new every day; get to bed sooner; exercise more often. Fold the answers and put them into a bucket (or similar).

Next, everyone who has written an answer writes down a question that they would like answered. When they have done this they sit in a circle and put the bucket in the middle. They then take turns to read their questions out to the whole class then pick an answer from the 'magic bucket' which they read aloud.

I am still not sure how this works but it does. Some of the answers are just fun but (more often than not) they link very closely to the question being asked.

The Backwards Walking Man

Key ideas:

How we 'orient' ourselves in life. The limitation we can impose upon ourselves by always doing things a certain way because we've always done them that way. How by changing our perspective we can 'turn ourselves around'.

One day Barbara and Ian were strolling along in the countryside when they came upon a most unusual sight. In the distance was a man who appeared to be walking backwards. He had an open rucksack across his shoulders and an intense look of concentration on his face. He was stooping low and seemed to be studying the ground very carefully.

'What *is* he doing?' Ian wanted to know. Barbara, practical as ever, said, 'Well, let's go and ask him shall we?'

As the children drew closer they saw that the man was picking up stones from the path and tossing them into his rucksack. It looked to be pretty full of rocks and pebbles of various sizes and must surely be quite a burden to bear.

'But why?' Ian began, when Barbara interrupted him with a shout.

'Look out!'

The backwards walking man had been so busy in his task that he'd failed to see a deep pothole behind him. Now, as he added another stone to his collection and took a further step backwards, his foot went into the hole and he toppled backwards and fell with a crash. Stones spilled out of his rucksack and the air gushed out of his lungs with a great whoosh. The children rushed up to help him.

'Here sir,' said Ian, 'let me give you a hand.' With Ian's assistance the man struggled to his feet while Barbara retrieved the rucksack, which had fallen from his shoulders, and laid it at his feet.

'Thank you indeed,' said the backwards walking man.

'You're very welcome,' Barbara replied. 'Although I suppose it must happen quite often if you don't look where you are going.' She did not mean to be rude and the man seemed not to be offended.

'Well,' he explained, 'I can see where I've been. And that's very important.'

'But why do you pick up the stones?' Ian blurted out.

The man looked serious. 'It's my path and I'm responsible for it. I can't have a stony path, can I now?'

'Paths always have stones on them,' Barbara said with a child's simple logic. 'And of course they can trip you up and get in your shoe and make walking uncomfortable. But that's just how stones are and there's no getting away from it!'

This gave the backwards walking man pause for thought. 'Hmm, there's something in that,' he pondered.

'And of course,' Ian chipped in, adding to what his sister had said, 'there will always be more stones along the way than you could possibly deal with. No one could ever collect them all and make the path perfectly smooth and safe.'

'Hmmm,' the man said again, his mind full of big thoughts now.

'So wouldn't it make better sense just to lay down your rucksack and take that weight off your shoulders?'

This idea was like a brilliant light to the man. His face glowed with happiness and he beamed a huge smile at the children. 'Thank you, thank you so much for helping me to see that. You're right! I'll simply leave that old rucksack where it is!'

So he did just that and, with a wave to Ian and Barbara, the man continued walking backwards on his way.

To do:

■ Discuss with the children what the story might mean.

■ Work with the class to create different stories that represent the idea of 'doing something a different way' and the consequences that can follow.

A Matter of Choice

Key idea:

We can choose our path through life. Young people are in a powerful position to do this.

Once upon a time in a land not so very far away there was an old man who lived in a big house all by himself. The house stood in huge and beautiful grounds, which were tended by a youth who came up from the village several times a week.

All his life the old man, whose name was Lee, had worked hard in the world of business and so made his fortune. His parents had been poor and lived in drudgery, and even as a young boy Lee decided that would never happen to him. Several times through the years he had grown rich and taken risks with his money and lost it all then gained it again. There had been a fire burning in him that would not be quenched by any quantity of jewels or gold. Because of his fierce ambition he had never married or cultivated true friends. Indeed, as he gazed through his window now he supposed that the boy who tended his garden was the closest friend he had.

That young man was called Jon. He had discovered years ago that he loved plants and was glad to have been employed by Lee, who paid him fairly for his work. Occasionally the old man came out to talk with him, of this and that, but nothing important beyond the company itself. Lee was here now, as Jon fetched a ladder from the shed and propped it against the house wall to trim the leaves of an ancient vine. They exchanged greetings, but the smile on the old man's face was rather wistful, even sad.

'I have discovered something through watching you,' Lee said. 'Look, you prop the ladder there and will climb it to trim the vine. My life has been like that too: I have climbed many rungs and reached the top. And here, high up, I gaze out over my years and my accomplishments.' Then Lee gave a brittle laugh and shook his head. 'But I realise now that I put the ladder against the wrong wall!'

'That is a hard thing to learn,' said Jon. 'But what if it were otherwise? What if the gods who look upon us could grant you a wish? What would you have – youth, beauty, power, a long life, the company of beautiful partners or any of the other glories we can imagine? But you may only have one of them. Choose now Lee, choose…"

To do:

The story can be discussed in terms of what our values are and the choices we can make.

Take it further:

There are many stories, traditional and contemporary, about making wishes and the consequences that follow. Ask the children to collect or recall some of these.

Teacher's note:

The metaphor of the ladder propped against the wrong wall appears in *The Way of Myth*, which is a transcript of conversations between the mythologist Joseph Campbell and Jungian analyst Fraser Boa. The motif of the gods granting but one wish comes from an account given by the philosopher Kierkegaard of an 'imaginary confrontation' he had with Mercury, the trickster god. Kierkegaard's choice was 'that I may always have the laugh on my side' (quoted in Larry Dossey, *Healing Beyond the Body*, p. 153).

Spirituality is a connection with something other, something deep. It could be a profound connection with the universe. It could be something which you have worked towards with your faith, religiously or non-religiously, such as Buddhism. Or even yoga. Again it is the connection with one self and your surroundings. Sometimes I comment on others that they are 'spiritual', these people tend to be quite grounded, calm, and in touch with their environment.

Arnie Hewitt

A Time for Everything

Key ideas:

One of the most important things we can learn – and pass on to children – is that it is good to have a sense of occasion. As demonstrated in this book, our lives can contain moments of sadness, seriousness, thoughtfulness – and silliness. We all like to be silly sometimes – but there's a time and place!

We went into the hall for assembly and sat quietly. There was some soft music playing – everybody was sitting listening to it – the whole school. So I sat down in my row and started to listen too. And then I don't know why, but I thought, 'What will happen if I make a really rude noise? A loud, rude noise. A really, really loud rude noise … the noise just like when you – well you know what I mean. And I'm good at that – making rude noises. Everybody would turn around and look. Everybody would laugh. The teachers would be mad – Mrs Mac would say "Jo – out!" And I'd be in real trouble – again … but hey … street cred!'

I'd heard that music before – loads of times – and I knew there was a quiet bit coming up where all the instruments went really soft and held on, before it went loud again. Perfect. So it got to the quiet bit and I looked around …

Everybody else was listening to the music, and they seemed to be enjoying it. It gave me a really nice feeling and then I thought: 'If I make a stupid noise, maybe it'll spoil it – and the music's not bad either. I listened to it for a bit longer thinking … shall I … shall I …?'

And then before I knew it Mrs Johnson – she's the deputy head – was saying 'Good morning everybody' and the assembly started. I'd missed it! And Mrs Johnson was saying, 'This is a passage from the Bible …

A time to be born, and a time to die;
a time to plant, and a time to pluck up what is planted;
a time to kill, and a time to heal;
a time to break down, and a time to build up;
a time to weep, and a time to laugh;

It was a time for listening – and thinking.

And then it was time to go out – and we went straight outside into the yard. And I made the loudest rude noise you can imagine. And all my mates laughed.

To do:

■ The passage is from the Old Testament (Eccles. 3:1–9). (The song 'Turn Turn Turn' recorded by The Byrds is based on this passage.) It continues:

A time to mourn and a time to dance;

A time to cast away stones and a time to gather stones together;

A time to embrace and a time to refrain from embracing;

A time to get and a time to lose;

A time to keep and a time to cast away;

A time to rend and a time to sew;

A time to keep silence and a time to speak;

A time to love and a time to hate;

A time of war and a time of peace.

◼ Discuss what you could add:

   ◆ A time to be stupid, a time to be serious.

   ◆ A time for playing football, a time for helping.

   ◆ A time for thinking about myself, a time for thinking about other people.

◼ Write and draw your own version of the verse from Ecclesiastes.

◼ Discuss why it is important for us to develop a sense of occasion; for example, to consider the feelings of others and the impact of our actions on them.

Take it further:

Rewrite the story from the point of view of another pupil, but this time imagine that the boy did make a stupid noise.

God for me means the essential goodness that I seek in every human being I meet. Sadly sometimes that goodness has been overlaid by pain and hurt, leading to anger and bitterness, but it is still there. Developing deep connection with, and between, other human beings is my spiritual path.

Belinda Hopkins

A Boy Ate a Chocolate Biscuit

A boy ate a chocolate biscuit. When the boy ate too much his mother said, 'You are going to turn into a chocolate biscuit.' So he went upstairs and he went inside the bedroom. And when he ate it he turned into a chocolate biscuit. When he woke up he was still a chocolate biscuit and when he tried to go to school he said to his mum, 'Mum my jacket won't go on.'

Story by Abdullah, aged 5

Illustration by Sebastian, aged 5

Activities

Slow Down!

Key ideas:

Looking at the links between the pace of life, time to think and developing spirituality.

There is a wise old saying in the literature of Zen Buddhism which tells us that 'sitting quietly, doing nothing – spring comes and the grass grows by itself'. The idea has many implications, some of them touched upon elsewhere in this book. The one I want to emphasise now is the notion of just *slowing down* (learning the health promoting art of doing nothing comes later).

What happens when many people sit quietly – or try to – is that their minds are still spinning, thinking of the 101 things that need doing now, or even sooner. At the back of such frantic mental activity is the uncritically accepted belief that doing nothing is a waste of time or even something to feel guilty about: the Devil makes work for idle hands and so on.

Of course, sitting quietly doesn't work given this state of mind. The act must be undertaken for its own sake, for the simple pleasure that it brings. And if the mind is going to whirl, then just let it whirl. In fact, settle back and watch it whirling. Allowing that is an early step in learning to meditate – watching the so-called 'monkey mind' scramble about in the tree of one's own imagined past and future. Watch the monkey while the grass grows by itself.

Slowing down brings physical benefits in terms of heart rate and pace of breathing, but the mind also quietens. It doesn't necessarily become passive or sluggish, but rather becomes more attuned to small, subtle or fleeting impressions that ordinarily we might miss. Applying the slow-it-down technique in the classroom works best if you've tried it yourself first. If you allow yourself just ten minutes of slow time a day (without watching the clock!), within a week you'll probably look forward to these brief sessions and relish them. In working with children, you might try the following…

To do:

- Start with short periods of slow-it-down and gradually increase the time; perhaps from a few minutes to five, ten or even longer if possible.

- Give the children something to do in the sessions: noticing their own breathing, looking at a painting or photograph, listening to some appropriate background music (so not thrash metal then), watching the world go by beyond the window.

Take it further:

- Combine slow-it-down with the idea of active meditation. Ask the children to look at, touch, smell and eat a piece of fruit and take ten minutes over it, savouring each moment.

- Read aloud a short poem (haiku are great for this) or short descriptive passage for the simple pleasure of hearing the flow of words rather than trying to work out any meanings.

- Have children do some simple act like sharpening a pencil – but slowly.

You're sure to think of many more ideas. Apart from the benefits already mentioned, slow-down time refreshes and energises the mind ready for the plunge back into our frenetic everyday world.

Links:

See Quiet Moments on page 34. An interesting read is *In Praise of Slow* by Carl Honoré.

> *Feelings of spirituality are rare and precious. They are sudden and unexpected glimpses of awareness and sometimes, clarity. They occur when my mind is clear of clutter. They leave me feeling moved and euphoric, and with a feeling of serenity that can last for some time.*
>
> **Diane**

Guided Fantasy – A Path to Meditation

Key idea:

To engage the imagination in a guided story where everyone's experiences will vary.

To do:

Ask participants to lie on their backs with their knees raised and their eyes shut. Ask them to feel the floor against their backs. Then ask them to imagine the floor is changing. It is becoming softer. It moves more easily and bends around them. Imagine the floor is no longer made of wood but it is becoming sand. Imagine feeling the sand between your fingers and it shaping itself around your body.

Imagine you are no longer in this room. You are lying on a beach. See yourself there. Hear the waves in the distance. And now I want you to imagine yourself standing up from the beach, breathing in the sea air and looking out at the ocean in front of you.

Think for a moment about what time of day it is. Is it night time or is it the day? What about the weather? Is it hot or cold, or is it windy or calm? Can you walk easily along the beach or do you have to battle your way against the wind? Have a look around you on the beach. Are there other people there or are you alone?

As you look around the beach, you see a raised area of land. Think about what you can see. Is it a hill, or is it more like a cliff, or mountains, or could it be some kind of man-made structure? Is it covered in grass or rocks, or is it smooth or jagged?

Start to walk towards the raised area. Finally reach it and look up. At the very top you see someone you need to reach. Who is it?

Think about how tall your raised area is. Will it be easy or difficult to reach the person?

However hard it is you find a way and begin to leave the beach and climb or walk up towards the top. Imagine yourself moving slowly or quickly upwards getting nearer and nearer to the person you want to reach.

You are just about to get there when you come across a strange hole that is big enough for you to climb into. You decide to explore and find yourself in a tunnel. Imagine yourself in the tunnel. Is it light or dark? Large or small? You start to move along the tunnel. Think about the walls on either side of you. Are they close or far apart? How long is the tunnel? Does it stretch on for miles or is it very short?

At the end of the tunnel you come to an enclosed area. What is it like? Is it a room or a cave? Can you see everything easily or is it in darkness? What are the walls like? Start to explore.

Suddenly on one of the walls you see a cupboard. You reach out your hand and open it. If for any reason it is locked you see a key hanging down from a hook. Use this key to open the cupboard. Inside the cupboard is an object. What is it? Pick up the object and hold it in your hand. Feel the weight of it. Explore it.

Suddenly you see a slope that leads out of the room and up to the top of the raised area. Take your object with you and walk up the slope as quickly as you can. At the top of the slope you find the person that you needed to reach. You give them the object. What do they do with it?

The person then gives you a message on a piece of paper. You open it and read it. You put the message in your pocket and return to the beach. You lie down on the sand and shut your eyes and think about the message. Slowly you come back to the room we are in. The sand becomes floor beneath you, and you can open your eyes and sit up in your own time.

- Invite pupils to share the message and who it was from with the rest of the group. (If pupils choose not to share their message they should not be forced.)

- Next give participants the chance to tell the story of their journey after all the messages have been heard.

We are more than we can know (as immeasurable as the Universe?); so, too, is 'God' (whatever we understand – or not – by that); so too are people we love, are used to, or prefer not to be near.

Canon Neville Boundy

Dealing with Feelings

Key idea:

Simple techniques combined with self-awareness can help us to manage our emotions.

Thoughts, emotions and the physical behaviour arising out of these are all connected. An important implication of this is that we can influence our feelings and actions through the power of the intellect and our creative imagination. Here are some techniques the children can practise immediately. I have found them to be very effective.

To do:

■ Positive Anchoring. An 'anchor' in this sense is a link that is created between a behaviour you want to do and something over which you have direct conscious control. A simple technique that I use goes like this. When I feel confident, happy, at ease and so on, I rub the thumb and little finger of my left hand together and say 'Calm and confident'. Each time I do this I strengthen the link between those feelings and that action. If I find myself in an uncomfortable situation, or if I'm feeling down, I perform the same action and say my little mantra. Usually triggering the positive anchor in this way helps me to feel better.

■ Multisensory Metaphor Game. If a child is bothered by an unpleasant feeling have him pretend it has a colour, makes a sound, has a shape, smell, texture, weight, heat… Represent the feeling in this way. Ask the child where it is inside. Then get the child to change every aspect of the feeling quickly – change its colour, shape, size and so on. Get the child to 'push' the feeling to some other part of his body. Then distract him – 'What time is it?' works well. Then say, 'How do you feel now?' The emotion may well have changed.

■ Positive Viewpoint. This is where you invite a child to consider the idea that all feelings, even unpleasant ones, can offer you something positive. Get the child to ask, 'What good thing is this feeling telling or giving me?' Suggest some examples. Anger could tell you that you have a strong sense of justice. You may want to act on that in a calm and confident way. Envy might tell you to look again at your values. Frustration might be a prompt to look for other ways to move forward.

■ Three Perceptual Positions. This is useful when children have opposing viewpoints. Arrange three chairs facing each other. The two children in disagreement each sit in a chair; the third is taken up by a 'neutral friend' whose job is to give the others a fair chance to speak their minds and, as necessary, to insist on mutual respect. After a time the two children in disagreement change places and discuss things from each other's viewpoint.

■ Timestrips. Take a long strip of paper (a till roll is ideal) and divide it up into sections. These might represent days, weeks, years and so on. Mark *now* on the strip. Then in the past write notes of apology; for example, what you wish you'd said, how you would act differently now. In the future write, draw and colour positive intentions, outcomes and affirmations.

Conflict Statues

Key idea:

This exercise is a great way to explore empathy for others.

Pupils will have the opportunity to portray and name emotions and look for resolutions. By modelling questioning along the lines of 'What does this character need in order to move on from the situation?' teachers will open up children's understanding of the fact that everyone has their own needs and each conflict has other sides to the one they might initially see.

Conflict arises out of unmet needs. When all our needs are being met we don't find ourselves in conflict. When we are able to articulate our needs, and accept that sometimes our needs can't be met at that time, then we begin to open ourselves up to higher intelligences.

To do:

- Stand in a circle as a whole class. They are going to learn five actions.

Action Number 1:	Pointing directly in front of you
Action Number 2:	Hands cupped by mouth which is open as if to shout
Action Number 3:	Both hands held over the mouth
Action Number 4:	Right hand on left shoulder, eyes looking at shoulder
Action Number 5:	Head down, looking at the floor

- Practise each of the moves until the group knows them off by heart. When you call 'Action Number 2' the group should quickly cup their hands by their mouth and look as though they are about to shout. Go through each of the numbers in various orders to make sure that they are familiar with them.

- Once everyone is happy they can remember the actions invite two pupils to come into the circle. Get them to stand slightly apart, with enough room to both point at each other and not touch. Then ask them both to face out so they are looking at the circle and not at each other.

- Ask if they have ever played Rock–paper–scissors. This part of the game is similar. Invite them to think of one of the five actions they have rehearsed. Count '1–2–3–Go' and on 'Go' the two pupils will turn and face each other frozen in the action that they have chosen. Instantly a conflict statue will appear in front of the group.

- Ask the class to get into pairs and have a few goes at this whilst you call out '1–2–3'. Maybe half the class works while the other watches and then swap. This way all the pupils can see how the conflict statues form and how even if two people choose the same action it still works as an image.

■ Once everyone has played with the actions, invite another two children into the centre of the group and calling out '1–2–3' get them to form a conflict statue. This time invite them to hold the image for a longer time. (If the subsequent conversation starts developing into a more extended enquiry with the rest of the class, remember to let these two rest their arms and then retake the statue posture once they are needed again.)

The conversation:

Ask the class what they see. You might want them to first talk objectively about what they can actually see: 'The girl is pointing at the boy who is looking at the floor.'

Next decide where the action has taken place. You might choose to set the scene on the school bus or in the dining hall. Or you may decide to let the group decide on the location. Once the location has been established find out from the class who the two characters are.

You can then ask them what they think has happened. This time they can be subjective in their response.

Explore a few possibilities, and then agree as a class on one scenario. Ask lots of questions to find out what has gone on. What are both people's role in the situation? Why are both characters doing what they are doing? Once the situation is established we want to find out from the class what each character is thinking in the situation.

Next we ask the class what each character is feeling in the situation.

Finally we ask what each character needs in order to move forward from the situation, or to resolve the situation.

Note:

You can move slowly through each stage with a different pair and a different conflict statue, inviting other children to experience the Rock–paper–scissors way of making images and taking time to explore each aspect of the questioning.

No Judgement Day

Key ideas:

Exploring what 'making a judgement' means. Looking at the difference between judgements and 'prejudgements' (prejudice). Realising that we are able to catch ourselves in the act of making judgements and control that behaviour for our own and others' benefit.

I recall somebody saying that one way to be happy is to stop having opinions. The same might be said about making judgements. Or rather making prejudgements, which is to say reaching conclusions based on insufficient knowledge and understanding. This tendency is the basis of the prejudice (from the Latin *praejudicium* meaning 'previous judgement, damage') that lies at the heart of many of the world's problems.

There was an advert on TV some years ago where a group of teenage boys were larking about in the street. One of them bumps into a woman walking to the car with her shopping and her purse falls to the ground. The boy snatches it up and – hands it back to her, with an apology for his and his friends' boisterousness. The advert was cleverly playing on the way that many viewers would automatically assume the youths had been intending to steal the woman's purse all along.

I have coined the term 'obserpinion' to describe an observation we make or something we experience, and an opinion we attach to it. Such an opinion is often automatic and just as frequently goes unchallenged by the person himself. If we fail to reflect on these opinions they can become generalisations and form a mental 'hardening of the categories'. Many such generalisations are also emotionally charged – they rouse the passions even before we have a chance to think further.

To do:

■ Consider the following statements in List 1. Decide whether or not you agree with them. Create similar statements for the children to think about, such as the ones in List 2.

■ Explain the idea of judgements and prejudgements. Discuss with children where their prejudgements might come from.

■ Do you agree with these statements?

List 1:

◆ The Welsh are more tight-fisted than the Scots.

◆ BMW drivers don't care about other road users.

◆ Italians make better ice cream than the English.

◆ The Prime Minister is doing a terrible job.

◆ Children were better behaved in the 1950s than they are now.

List 2:

◆ Football is a harder game than hockey.

◆ Twelve-year-old children understand more than 10-year-old children.

◆ Maths is difficult.

◆ Too much TV is bad for you.

◆ Pop songs were better in the old days.

If you decided yes (or indeed no) to any of these statements then I have made my point. Looking at any of the above more closely reveals that actually they are almost meaning-less – or at least beg many questions before we can come to any reasonable conclusion.

For example, what exactly is meant by 'the Welsh' or 'the Scots'? What if I was born in Wales but my family moved to England when I was a week old? What if both my par-ents were Scottish but settled in Wales ten years ago? What if… But you can probably think of plenty more scenarios for yourself.

Take it further:

One way of becoming more aware of obserpinions is to use a technique called Meta-Model questioning. Such questions attempt to elicit more details in challenging a generalisation by including terms such as *exactly, precisely, in more detail, further information* and so on:

■ What exactly do you mean by 'Welsh'?

■ How precisely are you defining 'tight-fisted'?

■ Explain further what you mean by the word 'better'.

■ Tell me more about what you mean by 'terrible'.

As you begin using this technique yourself, you will raise children's awareness of how com-mon and harmful generalisations and prejudging can be.

Gravity might keep my feet on the ground but spirituality keeps my heart in the right place.

Kresse

Moral Minitales

Key ideas:

How can we think further about what's right and wrong? Is morality absolute (God-given or wired into our genes), or does it depend upon the circumstances? Raising the notion of a 'dilemma' – a situation in which there is no ideal solution.

The word moral derives from the Latin meaning 'custom' while ethical, which is commonly thought to be the same thing, comes originally from the Greek *ethos* meaning 'character'. Indeed the *Concise Oxford Dictionary* defines moral as being concerned with character or disposition, and with the distinction between right and wrong. Both ideas involve an exploration of values, a necessary element in the development of spiritual awareness.

While many children 'know' what's right or wrong in any number of situations, examining why they think so and if they would act according to their beliefs is another matter. Inviting them to discuss ethical dilemmas creates the opportunity to reflect, compare their moral stance with others and think creatively in exploring the often relative nature of morality. This notion in turn touches upon the philosophical issue of whether a moral decision could ever be absolute; whether there is a 'buck stops here' baseline for deciding what is good or right and what is not.

To do:

Here are some ways of engaging children in discussing moral/ethical dilemmas…

■ Moral Minitales. Prepare a number of cards on which are written very brief situations for discussion. For example: 'You are on board a luxury liner which begins to sink. You manage to gain a place on a life raft with ten other people. But this is one too many and the raft starts to take on water. One person will have to leave the raft for the other nine to be saved. How do you choose who goes into the sea?'

Tip: The children will probably have lots of questions to ask, such as, Can everyone swim? Are any of the passengers children? Are there sharks in the water? and so on. Flip a coin to get an answer. Later, ask the children if or how their decisions would differ if the coin had said yes instead of no at certain points in the discussion.

■ Write or draw you dilemma and possible solutions to it in the boxes. Then discuss the order 'rightness' of the different solutions and write which option you chose – and why!

■ What-if dilemmas linked to topics and subject areas. For instance: 'What if global warming meant that the wealthy nations (including ours) could only help poorer countries by cutting its standard of living by 50%? This means you have to give up half of what you've got. What would you personally sacrifice? What should the nation give up? And why?'

Tip: Such a discussion can be preceded by research so that children are armed with some facts, figures and scientific opinion. What-if scenarios can be explored by asking three subsidiary questions:

◆ What would the world be like?

◆ What problems would arise?

◆ How might we solve the problems?

■ A choice of solutions. Create dilemmas and offer the children some options for resolving them. Ask the groups to put their choices in rank order, with reasons for the priority added. For example, you see a person illegally dumping toxic waste in a rarely visited wood. Do you:

◆ Challenge the person on the spot and tell him to stop?

◆ Go straight to the police?

◆ Ask the person for money to keep your mouth shut?

◆ Go home because it's not your problem anyway?

What is spirituality? It might be creatively allowing the unexpected, unwanted, uncomfortable, the as-yet-unknown a space in which to be felt.

Canon Neville Boundy

Would You Rather ...?

Key ideas:

An exploration of our wishes and desires and a chance to reflect on values and those of our peers.

The Would You Rather? game is often used as a Philosophy for Children exercise. It is possible to adapt this exercise for use with children of all ages.

■ Write statements on the five blank cards to make your own set of 'Would You Rather?' cards.

■ Place the Would You Rather? card on the floor in the centre of your group. Then slowly place the other cards around it:

   ◆ Earn a million pounds

   ◆ Win a major TV talent show

   ◆ Put an end to world poverty

   ◆ Wake up with a super power

   ◆ Have your own TV show

Give your class time to think and then they walk to the one that best suits them. Once they are standing by the card that suits them give each group a chance to discuss why they chose that card and what it means to them.

Allow this to develop into a discussion. Would they change their minds? How do they answer the differing views of others in the group?

■ Next, place pupils into groups of four or five and ask them to create a series of Would You Rather? cards. Each group is given a type of person or group of people to aim their cards at:

   ◆ Group 1: Children under age of 7

   ◆ Group 2: Older people (75+)

   ◆ Group 3: Teachers

I have had great questions set by pupils for the Teachers group, such as, 'Would you rather teach a group who were well behaved in the morning but awful after dinner, a class who never behaved well but laughed at all your jokes, or a class who passed all their exams but were a bit boring?'

   ◆ Group 4: Year 6 about to leave primary school

   ◆ Group 5: A football team about to play against a side in a higher league

   ◆ Group 6: A group of extremely rich people

■ Once groups have created their questions invite them to lead the Would You Rather? session, putting the rest of the class in roles as the people they have aimed their questions at.

The Mundane and the Sacred

Key ideas:

That spiritual intelligence develops by realising that we carry it inside ourselves. Becoming more spiritually aware can happen in our ordinary lives, without having to go to some special place. Simply waiting for spiritual experiences to happen isn't as effective as deciding that what is sacred is all around us.

One facet of spiritual intelligence is the ability to appreciate that whatever motivates and gives meaning to the universe goes beyond words; it is ineffable, not able to be spoken about. Or as Carl Jung said, it is numinous – surpassing comprehension. An awareness of this goes hand in hand with an acceptance of it and being able to feel comfortable with it. Also, spiritually intelligent people realise that because everything is actually all-one-thing, then the sacred is to be found everywhere, in the smallest and most mundane of objects, situations and experiences.

The tradition of oral storytelling contains a beautiful metaphor summed up by the idea that 'telling stories is like climbing a ladder to the moon' (see http://www.crickcrackclub.com/ CRICRACK/ARTLADRF.HTM). Without wishing to misrepresent what other people mean by this, for me the image sums up the connections that exist between the 'earthiest' of stories – gossip, neighbourhood tales, local news items – and myths of the gods and the creation of the cosmos. In other words there is a direct line from where we are grounded in the here-and-now to the eternal and infinite heavens.

Eastern spiritual traditions have long recognised the importance of the ordinary in appreciating what is sacred; and to me this is the most sensible way of speaking about what goes beyond words. Thus it is that Hui Neng, a central figure in Buddhist history, advises that, 'If somebody asks you a question about ultimate reality, always answer in terms of everyday. If they ask you about everyday life, answer in terms of ultimate reality.'

To do:

■ To get a flavour of this, try the following game. Write down six Big Questions about 'the meaning of it all' and six simple statements about ordinary things. Roll a dice to select one of the questions, then roll again to pair it with a simple statement. For example:

List 1: Big questions

1. What is my purpose in life?

2. What is the nature of my soul?

3. How can I find God?

4. How can I live a more spiritual life?

5. Where is the proof that God exists?

6. Why is there evil in the world?

List 2: Simple statements

1. We've had lots of rain this summer.

2. Earlier I saw my cat chasing a butterfly.

3. I will give my best friend a call tonight.

4. In two days time there will be a full moon.

5. Look, a plastic cup blowing along the street.

6. I hear children playing in the park.

I got 'How can I live a more spiritual life?' and 'We've had lots of rain this summer'. Now there are various ways I can work with this. I can try to analyse how summer rain is a metaphor (but see 'Koan, Koan – Gone' on page 16), I can put it down as a bit of New Age gobbledygook (When the evening star touches the mountain peak the spirit of the disciple is ready, Grasshopper), or I might do as Alan Watts suggests and consider that a spiritual life and summer rain are one and the same thing.

Spirituality invites us to be ready to think, pray, feel, imagine afresh; it encourages us to be uncluttered and allow the apparently already familiar to comfort and challenge anew.

Canon Neville Boundy

Get Real!

Key ideas:

To explore what it means to be real. The importance of authenticity and being present.

It is all too easy for children (and adults) to lose a sense of reality amidst the constant bombardment of alternatives to real life: interactive games, 3D films and endless possibilities for fantasy to be found on the Internet. This plethora of platforms for unreality can sometimes overwhelm our senses and the day-to-day joy of recognising our own uniqueness and the potential in each moment.

This exercise is about bringing the child back to a place of self-discovery and curiosity about who they are, where they are and who they are with.

To do:

■ Sit the children in a circle on the floor so that they are comfortable, and spend a few moments getting them into a relaxed state. You probably have several techniques for doing this but if not try the following:

◆ Ask the children to sit or lie down and to place their right hand on their chest and their left hand on their stomach.

◆ Ask them to breathe out then breathe in to a slow count of three noticing that when they breathe in the air goes into their tummy (left hand) first and then their chest (right hand) second.

◆ Hold the breath for two seconds and breathe out with the chest (right hand) deflating first and the tummy (left hand) deflating second.

◆ Rest for two seconds before breathing in. Repeat the process at least five times then begin the exercise.

■ Keeping their eyes closed (and their breathing steady) ask them to imagine their right hand. What does it look like? How big is it? Does it have any marks, scratches, scars? What do their nails look like?

■ Once you have talked the children through recalling their hand ask them to keep their eyes closed but to hold their hand up in front of their closed eyes and ask them again to recall it. Now that they have their hand in front of their faces (even though their eyes are closed) has this helped them to recall and provide greater detail?

■ Next ask them to open their eyes and quietly look at their hands. Did they have a clear picture of their hands in their heads? Is there something significant about their hands that they had never noticed before?

■ Ask them now to describe to each other what is happening beneath the skin. How is it structured? How does it work? Once the children have discussed this with each other open up the dialogue to include the whole group.

■ Finally, ask them if there are any other things about themselves or others or the day-to-day world that, if they took a little time to stop and notice, could reveal something to them that would make them think or bring them joy. For example, a spider's web that still has morning dew clinging to it or sunlight through their bedroom window.

■ What are the benefits to them of stopping and slowing down?

Take it further:

■ In pairs, sitting back to back, ask one child to describe the other – what they are wearing, what they look like and so on. Once they have both done this they are to turn and face each other. Did they not include something that was obvious (colour of the other person's hair, eyes or shoes)? Did they include something that was not there?

■ Ask the children to close their eyes and describe the environment that they are in. Having described it with their eyes closed ask them to look around and see what they had not noticed and check what they had included that was only in their imagination.

■ How much does our imagination create things in our mind that are not really there?

■ Do we sometimes act on what we *think* and not what we *know*?

■ How can we make sure that we say and do things that are based in reality and not fantasy?

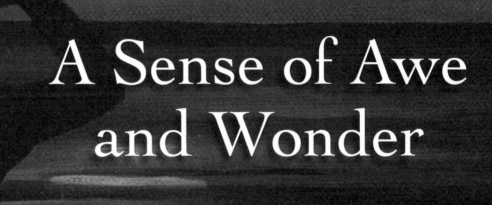

A Sense of Awe
and Wonder

Stories

First Light

Key ideas:

We are surrounded by moments of devastating beauty, awe and wonder. When we create space to observe and experience these moments we can begin to see them more often and in numerous, unexpected places.

Holidays were always exciting in our house partly because we had so few of them. With a family of seven children (six boys and one girl) it meant there was little spare cash to spend on trips away. Our school holiday usually consisted of days in the park or trips to aged relatives. Not that I am complaining. I loved the park. It had a huge stomach-turning slide, see-saws and swings as well as a public paddling pool (long since closed for health and safety reasons).

I did not mind visiting my older relatives as they provided nice food, love and the occasional bit of low currency cash. No, holidays at home were fine. But when we had our first family holiday I thought we had entered a world of adventure, magic and amazement.

Getting on holiday required us all to pile into a minibus that my Dad had been able to pick up for a bargain price. The smell of diesel fumes throughout the journey was an indication of why the vehicle was so cheap. We helped to pack numerous suitcases in various stages of decay and watched my Dad risk life and limb by clambering on top of the tank-green van to attach bags, tent and other camping necessities to a roof rack that a friend had loaned him for the journey. My mother was not convinced that it would stay on the roof but my father reassured her by binding everything down with orange nylon rope. By the time he had finished you could barely make out the suitcases under the black plastic bags and frenzy of orange twine.

We all clambered into the van and the journey began. It was an uneventful journey apart from the one moment of drama when I became dramatically car sick and shared the contents of my stomach with my sister and one of my brothers. After stopping at a service station on the English–Welsh border to freshen up the minibus and clean up sickly children we continued on our quest to the Welsh coast.

We arrived after several uncomfortable hours made more challenging by the very hot weather and no air-conditioning. It was late afternoon by the time we had set up the tent and unpacked the van. After a meal of instant mashed potato, tinned beans and sausage (this was to become an almost daily mealtime delight) my father suggested that we take our coats and take the ten minute walk from the campsite to the beach. Fantastic! Late night. Beach. Sea. What could be better?

Ice cream! Just before the beach there was an ice cream kiosk in the final stages of closing. My father treated us all to an ice cream with strawberry sauce, a chocolate flake and hundreds and thousands scattered on top.

We could hear the sea and ran across the still warm sand to see who could see the sea first, careful not to tip our over-laden ice cream from its precarious wafer base.

It was getting to the end of a warm and tiring day and the light was beginning to fade. We all sat, like a gang of ice cream eating goblins, watching the waves crash onto the beach. It was one of the very rare occasions that all of my family were together and there was no noise. There was just the sound of the sea and the occasional crunching of wafers.

'Look at that,' my Dad said pointing to the sky.

The dark blue of the sky was mixing with the rippling shape of the clouds and the last fierce rays of the sun to create a dappled effect the like of which I had no memory of till that moment.

'That's a mackerel sky,' said my Dad.

'Why is it called that?' asked a child's voice.

'Is it because there are mackerel in the sea and the sky is over the sea?' someone else asked.

'No, it's because the colour and pattern of the sky is similar to the colour and pattern of a mackerel's skin.' My Dad was a keen weekend fisherman and knew these things.

There was a collective 'Ohhh …' and then silence.

Darkness soon followed and we made our way across the fields, giggling and giddy with joy and too much sugar, whilst my eldest brother was given the job of shining a huge industrial-sized torch on the ground ahead of us to light our way.

If you have ever spent a night in a middle sized tent which consisted of two flimsily partitioned bedrooms and one galley area (where myself and two more of my brothers slept along with the stove, food and most of the world weary suitcases) you know the hysteria that getting ready for bed in these cramped conditions can create.

Finally, when we were all settled down and zipped into our maroon sleeping bags like huge and repulsive slugs my father asked my brother to pass the light to him. On the inside wall of my father's canvas bedroom shone a powerful white light that acted like a large round cinema screen. My father then spent the next twenty minutes making shapes with his hands and creating the silhouettes of birds, dogs, elephants and faces (including a very scary witch). He told us stories (of a witch with a cat that caught a bird and a dog and ended up being crushed by an elephant).

When the light went out it was totally dark. It was a darkness you only find in the countryside. In the silence we could hear the hooting of an owl and the occasional voices of merry tent dwelling folk.

It had been a long day like no other I had ever experienced. I lay there happy and amazed at all that we had squeezed into the first day of our first holiday.

I could not wait until tomorrow as I had promised my two galley sleeping brothers that we would get up early and make our way down to the beach to watch the first light on the clouds. We wanted to see if a mackerel sky is something that happens every day or was it something that happened just on special days. Days like today.

To do:

This activity is simple but profound in bringing awe and wonder from the 'then and there' to 'here and now'. It could be done as a single lesson or spread out over days or even weeks.

■ Show a picture of an image from space that reflects the vastness of the universe. Ask the questions: What is amazing about this picture? What questions or statements come to mind? How does it make you feel? Does it make you want to do anything?

■ Next show a picture of the Earth from space. Ask the same questions.

■ Next show some images of the power of nature: earthquakes, birds in flight, lightning and so on. Ask the same questions.

■ Now bring the image closer to home. You may have an aerial picture of the town or city where you school is. Again, ask the same questions.

■ Finally, ask the students to look around the school grounds and photograph images that are full of awe and wonder and then ask them to return and share their images.

Take it further:

■ What were their first memories of something that made them amazed – something truly wonderful?

■ Have the children complete the 'First Light' worksheet.

■ Can we find things to be amazed about wherever we are or only in special places and at special times?

Spirituality is the feeling of awe and wonder when you look at a beautiful flower or a wild ocean. It's listening to a piece of music and feeling your heart swell. It's appreciating the beauty of a moment.

It's knowing that we are all tiny, fleeting specks in this vast universe, and yet all unique and significant and capable of great things.

It's allowing our spirit to guide and enrich us, to be all that we can be in the fullest sense of living.

Pauline Milligan

There's Nothing There!

Key ideas:

In our busy lives, when we're always rushing to see the next thing, sometimes it's good to stop and look around. With our superficial glances, we often miss the beautiful – and the fascinating. It's far too easy to say 'there's nothing there'. Often, the longer you look, the more you'll see.

We walked down to the bottom of our garden to where the old orchard had turned into a wilderness overgrown with elders, nettles, brambles and sticky goose grass. 'There's nothing here,' I said. But we sat on the bench anyway, just sitting in the woods at the bottom of the garden.

I looked around at the ancient apple trees, old and gnarled – the stained brown branches, where the bark had fallen off, were dotted with tiny holes. Some of the leaves, even though they were green, were a bit curled at the edges and had some black spots on them. Tiny hard fruits were emerging through withered petals, invisibly swelling until in the autumn they'd fall as sweet and juicy apples the size of a tennis ball.

And the cow parsley! Five feet tall – like flowery white lacy umbrellas.

A tiny bird, a wren – or maybe a goldcrest – darted and jumped and flitted so fast that I thought I knew what colour it was – but I wasn't quite sure.

From high above came a drilling, stuttering noise as a woodpecker attacked a dead branch. I strained my eyes, peering up into the dark stems silhouetted against the milky blue sky. And finally I caught a glimpse of his shuddering green–brown body.

Something rustled in the bramble patch behind us. I didn't turn around, but my imagination began to run wild. A fat, mottled baby blackbird jumped out onto the path, hopping and staring, cocking its head to aim a beady, inquisitive eye at the two of us.

I looked again at the trees and plants around me. So many shades of green and brown, no two the same. I leant down to pick a dandelion flower with its straight lines of yellow shooting out from the centre. The stem had tiny white whiskers and I squashed it between my fingers until a nasty smelling liquid oozed out and stained my fingers.

A spider's web glistened with tiny droplets of water, reflecting the rainbow sunlight which dappled around me, casting onto the ground the ever-moving shadow patterns of leaves which danced high above my head.

We sat as the woodland morning happened around us. And then we got up and walked back towards the trampoline. 'You see,' I said, 'there's nothing there …'

To do:

You could ask the children to:

- Take time to look and write down or draw the things they see and hear. You could use a photograph or film – but filling the senses with a real environment is so much better if it's possible. On a river bank, on top of a hill, looking out to sea, looking into a rock pool, in a park.

- Try sitting and looking for about ten minutes and then write down key words to describe what they notice. Think about what they see, smell, hear and feel.

- To focus the activity try 'The five most interesting things I saw'.

- Try recording a minute's sequence of natural sounds. Again you could focus on 'The five most interesting things I heard'. You could use this (looped) to recreate an atmosphere in the classroom.

- Ask the children to create a response to the environment they have observed in the way they feel most comfortable with. It could be free verse, 'myku' (see page 119), a sound picture (which may or may not include rhythmic elements), a piece of descriptive prose, a drawing or painting, a piece of movement.

Take it further:

■ Encourage children's curiosity by showing them how to find out more about the things they are surrounded by – the names of trees, plants and birds and how living things are all different and unique – like us!

■ Explore the life cycles of plants – how and why fruits are produced.

■ Rather than destroying the mystery, often the closer you look and the more you know and understand – the more you realise how miraculous and fascinating something is. Look at colours in nature – copy some shades of green and make your own colour sample card with small squares of green shades (like a paint colour matching card from a DIY shop). Give each shade a name, perhaps by taking the plain names of the rainbow colours – red, orange, yellow and so on – and adding adjectives or descriptive phrases to 'pin down' the colours more surely. (This could be linked to How to Bury a Rainbow activities on pages 89–90.)

■ Take a natural object such as a flower, a twig or a leaf. Make a really detailed series of drawings or paintings of it. Again, the closer you look the more you'll see.

Spirituality is the realisation that I am part of something great and enduring. I am small, and my time is short but I feel a sense of belonging. When I touch something ancient, or experience the wonder of trees, mountains, oceans, stars, the cycle of life and death, I feel connected to the all that has gone before me and all that is yet to come. I feel connected to the universe itself.

Diane

The Ladybirds

Key ideas:

The differences we see in the world are all part of a greater unity. Everything is interdependent – the sky is enhanced by the presence of clouds, clouds are given meaning by reference to the sky. This idea applies at all levels – without darkness we could not appreciate light.

One day Susan was playing in the garden. The morning had been wet and thundery, but now the sun was shining warmly down on her as she ran here and hid there and noticed all kinds of things for the first time.

After some minutes she came across two ladybirds on a leaf. They were locked in what looked like a fierce struggle, rolling this way and that but never breaking apart – each trying to gain mastery over the other. Both of the ladybirds were strikingly different from any that Susan had ever seen before. One was pure white with a single black dot in the middle of its back. The other was pure black, and in the centre of its back was a solitary white spot. Very unusual, Susan thought.

Susan liked the look of the white ladybird, for it seemed clean and pleasant and kind of sunny like the afternoon was turning out to be. On the other hand the appearance of the black ladybird frightened her rather. It looked sinister, menacing and evil.

As she had these thoughts Susan continued to watch the two insects in their pointless battle. Sometimes the subtle balance tipped and the black ladybird rolled over on top of its white opponent. Then after some seconds of effort the tables were turned and the white ladybird managed to gain the advantage. But soon after the black enemy, with a renewed burst of strength, became dominant again.

Susan decided that she had better do something about this before the white ladybird was harmed – or even killed!

She reached out to separate the two struggling creatures, but found they could not be moved apart. No matter how hard she tried she was unable to pull the white one free, so closely and tightly was it intertwined with the black.

Susan tried again and again, but to no effect. She became so engrossed in her mission that she failed to notice black clouds piling up again in the sky as the rainy weather returned – until at last a rumble of thunder alerted her.

She looked up, very frightened at first but then relieved to see that the strong winds of change were still blowing and the storm was coming to nothing after all. The clouds were sliding away to let the sun once more shine brilliantly down.

And then, understanding something important, she let the ladybirds alone, because the force that bound them was no different from that which made the day and the night, summer and winter, life and death, the stars and the spaces between them.

To do:

■ What could the 'force' be that binds the ladybirds? How is that connected to day and night, summer and winter, and so on?

■ Link the story to 'Looking at Symbols' (see page 95). How does the situation involving the ladybirds link with what we take the yin–yang symbol to mean?

Take it further:

■ The story suggests that all things have to exist together. This includes the idea that evil exists – and has to exist – not only so that we can appreciate goodness but also choose for ourselves how to behave in life.

■ Complete the worksheet to list good and evil things.

■ Could a good and perfect world ever exist?

■ If evil is going to happen anyway why should we try to stop it?

■ In Christianity, God is all-seeing and all-powerful. Why doesn't He stop evil from happening?

■ What does 'evil' mean? And what is 'goodness'?

Once There Was a Unicorn

Once there was a unicorn who lived next to a waterfall in a really sunny forest. One day a strange man came to the forest looking for the unicorn. The unicorn hid behind the waterfall so the man couldn't find her. The man wanted to take the unicorn away but the waterfall wanted the unicorn to stay. So it summoned all its strength, became really powerful and washed the man away.

Story by Lauren, aged 5

Illustration by Djellza, aged 6

Activities

How Do You Bury a Rainbow?

Key idea:

Looking deeper at natural phenomena and using this as stimuli to explore myths and legends that have been inspired by these across the centuries.

Yesterday a rainbow died on our street
Now oily dye discards discoloured stains on gravelled ground
I watch,
Wanting to wash away a washed out spectrum from its grey grave
But how do you bury a rainbow?

Since the beginning of time, people have been looking at rainbows with a sense of awe and wonder. The rainbow features in many mythologies as generation after generation create myths and legends to explain this remarkable natural phenomenon.

In medieval Germany there was a belief that no rainbow would appear in the sky for forty years before the end of the world. They even had a saying about it: 'So the rainbow appears, the world has no fear, until thereafter forty years.'

In Greek mythology, the rainbow was thought to be the path made by Iris, messenger of the gods, on her journeys between heaven and Earth.

In Christianity the rainbow serves to represent the promise between God and Noah that he will never again destroy the world with flood. This same theme occurs in the Epic of Gilgamesh, where the rainbow is described as the jewelled necklace of the goddess Ishtar, which she hangs in the sky to serve as her promise never to forget the days of the great flood.

In many cultures, there is a recurring assertion that the rainbow is a symbol of the god's anger being abated. There are also numerous references across mythologies to the rainbow serving as a multicoloured bridge between heaven and Earth.

In Europe stories of pots of gold and leprechauns abounded, and the impossible journey to the end of the rainbow fuelled the sense of mystery as to what could be hidden there.

The rainbow has been referred to as the 'Pathway of Souls' by Native Americans, and the 'Floating Bridge of Heaven' by the Japanese, and many cultures believed that the rainbow was used to transport the spirit of the good up to the afterlife. (See 'Myths and Legends about Rainbows' by Amy E. Davies at http://nides.bc.ca/Assignments/Weather/Legends. htm)

To do:

■ People in the past have made strong spiritual connections to the sighting of a rainbow. Maybe it is time to look again at this natural phenomenon with our modern day eyes.

■ What is the new mythology behind the rainbow? What purpose, if any does it serve in our times?

■ Involve your class in investigating the myths and stories that have arisen to explain the rainbow.

■ Engage your class in collecting pictures of rainbows in the sky and rainbows in puddles. Are there other places that rainbows form naturally (e.g. mother of pearl)? Use the pictures to stimulate debate about the sense of awe a rainbow can inspire.

■ Once your class have gathered myths and pictures ask them to explore what they have in common and create lists of the aspects the myths share and aspects that stand alone.

■ Use this information to create a class rainbow myth for the twenty-first century.

■ Look at the oily rainbow picture and discuss what happens when a rainbow dies.

■ In woodland or on a beach look for natural objects which show the colours of the rainbow. On a beach you could make a 'rainbow' from shells, seaweed, stones and so on.

■ Use the rainbow frame to write a rainbow myth, or a poem, with a line describing each colour.

I Wonder Why?

Key ideas:

Asking questions is where a lot of thinking starts. Sometimes we can't explain the things we see and the word 'wonder' has to change sense – from a question to a statement. We just can't know everything about the world around us – instead we stand amazed at the wonder of it.

I wonder why the sky is blue
I wonder why the sea is too
I wonder why the grass is green
And why a rainbow can be seen.

I wonder if the stars at night
So far away and yet so bright
Have life on them – is there a plan?
… And how the universe began.

I wonder why I'm here today.
Why do I say the things I say?
What makes me, me? What makes you, you?
And why, when you smile, I smile too!

To do:

■ Think about the meaning of the word 'wonder'. It can have two meanings. We often use it as a verb in a question: I wonder if …, I wonder what …, I wonder why … But wonder as a noun also means something amazing or remarkable – a miracle – perhaps something that can't be explained. And used in this sense, as a noun, wonder can mean to be filled with wonder – at something wonderful – or wondrous. It comes from the Old English word *wundor* (you'll find it in the hymn of Cædmon on page 108).

■ Read the lyrics of the song 'I Wonder' and think of some more 'I wonder why' questions. You could develop these into a group or class poem, with individuals either suggesting ideas as the teacher scribes, or by asking the children to write a line, couplet or a verse themselves (depending on ability). These could then be put together to form the whole poem or song.

■ Think about the world we live in and ask some questions you don't know the answers to.

Take it further:

The scientific method often begins with a question, followed by a hypothesis which is then tested and conclusions drawn. You can ask other people questions – or you can ask yourself a question – to try to make sense of something. But sometimes we can't think of the answer. Ask pupils to think of a question to which the answer can be explained. Then ask them to think of a question to which the answer can't be explained. Much thought and discussion should ensue!

I Wonder

Key idea:

Wonderment is a natural part of children's development. We can nourish this in simple ways.

I recall a Chemistry teacher in a school where I worked – Mr Perkins or Perko to both staff and pupils alike (though not to his face). I remember him particularly for two things he said. On one occasion, in the middle of a heated staffroom discussion on how far teachers should be responsible for the 'pastoral care' of children, Perko said, 'Well I just intend to be a caring presence to them and have them know they can come to me for help whenever they like.' Another time we were listening to some news on the radio, again in the staffroom, when Perko turned to us and said, 'Isn't it a wonderful thing?' We said, 'What?' 'The radio,' he replied. 'I mean, even though I know how it works, it's still wonderful.' And you could see it in his eyes too, that look of wonderment.

Children's natural curiosity spontaneously gives rise to wonderment. As a noun it encompasses feelings akin to astonishment, puzzlement, even elation, with perhaps a pinch of frustration at not knowing the answer. As a verb – to wonder – it evokes endless questions and the search for knowledge. Even when we do know we can still be held in wonder; when we don't know our wonderment generates a profound appreciation of things and a gladness that we are around to witness the world.

In *The Educated Mind*, Professor Kieran Egan of Simon Fraser University suggests that children progress through several levels of understanding on their way to adulthood. Young children display a *mythic understanding* characterised in part by comprehending the world through stories. These are explanations that children create or hear and accept for events and phenomena they don't understand. For instance, 'thunder is only the clouds bumping together' is how my parents explained thunder to allay my fears. Slightly older children (upper Key Stage 2 into Key Stage 3) evolve a *romantic understanding*, where mythic stories are tested and limits are sought. Such understanding includes 'fascination…with the limits of reality, and pervasive wonder'. Romantic understanding is characterised by an ongoing sense that the world is wonderful, coupled with a search for limits and boundaries, in order to create a 'reasonable' understanding of how the world works.

When I think of this I'm reminded of what the writer Alan Garner said, that people are like onions – we all have layers. So as adults we still have the capacity to wonder and to model that attitude for children to feel safe in being like that too.

To do:

Practically you can encourage wonderment by:

- Sprinkling your lessons with what's called 'gee whiz' ideas: facts and concepts that make you go 'Wow!' Thousands of these can be found for example in the *Guinness Book of Records* or simply by doing an Internet search. One of my favourite wows is the (not entirely proven) fact that the largest dinosaur ever was Seismosaurus – Earthquake Lizard – that has been claimed to grow to 148 feet, nearly half the length of a football field!

- Using the technique of *vivid particularities*. These can be fictional or factual details that evoke vivid mental images and have an emotional impact. For instance, I read recently in a book about the Sutton Hoo ship burial that the carapace of a ladybird was found perfectly preserved amongst some cloth. It had crawled into the grave ship and never crawled out. Another vivid detail that has stuck in my mind for years is the image of the poet John Keats waking with a fit of coughing and noticing a spot of blood on his white pillow. His training as an apothecary led him to know by the colour of the blood that he had TB, which proved fatal the following year (1821). Keats died aged 26.

- Displaying quotations that celebrate wonderment. For example, Albert Einstein said: 'There are only two ways to live your life. One is as though *nothing is a miracle*. The other is as though *everything is a miracle*.'

- Ask the children to draw or write about three things that make them say wow!

Incidentally, but aptly, the origin of the word miracle is 'to wonder at' and has links with the Sanskrit *smayate*, 'he smiles'.

'Going Yourself'

Key idea:

We can't help but express our uniqueness, but we can influence how we do it.

The title could have been written more clearly as 'being yourself', but the choice was determined by the idea that all of life is process and flow rather than being a 'state', something discrete and static, separate and named. The Victorian Jesuit poet Gerard Manley Hopkins coined the terms *inscape* and *instress* in an attempt to explore this profound and yet obvious insight.

Inscape could be thought of as the uniqueness of each and every created thing, its 'individual landscape' reflecting the divinity that gives it expression. Instress is, I think, both the act of that expression and the creative tension existing between the interaction of all things; all things expressing themselves – what in Taoism is referred to metaphorically as 'the ten thousand things', this being an illusion of the senses hiding the true unity of all. Another way of thinking about it is to say that the creative force of the universe 'sprays out' an infinite variety of forms, all undeniably and uniquely themselves, but all reflections of their common origins. This is beautifully summed up in a line I once heard from a film (I forget which), where one character says to another, 'The features by themselves aren't important, it's the spirit animating them that matters.'

For Hopkins and many other spiritual thinkers, everything is in flux, everything flows – or 'goes along'. When that flowing-of-existence expresses a thing's individuality it is 'going itself', expressing its own uniqueness. Another term Hopkins used to describe this is 'selving', which means something not just being itself but constantly expressing itself through life. His poem 'As kingfishers catch fire…' explores the idea beautifully.

The philosopher Alan Watts throws further light on this when he says that it makes sense to ask not what an apple tree is but what it does – and the answer is 'it apples', in the same way that a stream streams or a sky skies, the summer summers or a learner learns. Interestingly the educationalists Neil Postman and Charles Weingartner wonder why 'mind' tends to be used as a noun, suggesting that we could more accurately regard it as a verb: the mind as a thing is misleading – we are constantly engaged in the act of 'minding'.

To do:

- Encourage children to play the game of turning nouns into verbs to highlight the perception of life-as-flow.

- Discuss what it means to 'selve', to express one's unique self. Kittens can't help but kitten; thinking people have choice. What can we *do* to best express who we are?

- Hopkins used other techniques to describe uniqueness, including alliterative word combinations such as fawn-froth (the froth on a tumbling stream), dapple-dawn-drawn falcon, couple-colour, silk-sack clouds, the dare-gale skylark. Brainstorm further examples with the group: in one class I worked with Ellen said that the kitten loves to 'powderpuff-tumble' with its brothers and sisters.

I feel most in touch with my spiritual core when I am alone and outside – preferably in the wild. However wherever there is natural beauty, and it is everywhere when I look for it, I can touch base with the magic and mystery of creation.

Belinda Hopkins

Looking at Symbols

Key idea:

Symbols are a way of gathering together all sorts of thoughts, feelings and meanings. We can look at a symbol without having to analyse it. On the other hand, it can remind us of so many things.

The word symbol derives from Ancient Greek for 'to throw together'. I think of this as a bringing together into one representation of many layers of meaning. The philosopher Alan Watts suggests that symbols 'point beyond themselves' to ideas and experiences that may ultimately leave words, images or rational thought itself behind.

Symbols become more powerful over time: they 'accumulate significance' through being interpreted in many ways and being absorbed into and modified by various cultures. Religious symbols are among the most influential, with huge emotional energy being attached to them.

To do:

You can help children to appreciate the power and value of symbols by trying these activities.

- Show the group a symbol such as the yin–yang below. Ask: 'What could it be? What does it remind you of?' Once some ideas have been generated challenge the children further by asking: 'If this picture said something about how we can live a happier life, what do you learn?' In other words, have the children think for themselves before 'telling them the answer' of what the symbol actually means.

- Use simple abstract designs to encourage the children to think creatively, interpret for themselves and 'add meaning'. Use the pattern of questioning above. Here are a few images to get you started.

  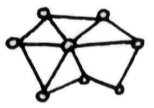  

Take it further:

- Invite the children to invent symbols for themselves through their own bodies. Examples invented by one class include –

◆ Finger points to myself – means this is where I can find answers.

◆ A circle of outspread hands – means working together we can solve problems.

◆ Two children holding hands, leaning away from one another – means mutual support.

■ Ask the children to draw their symbol in the top half of the frame and write their meaning in the bottom half. You could cut out the frames, separating the two halves and use them as a class or group matching game to stimulate discussion about the meanings .

■ A simple but effective way of creating symbols is to make a word grid like the one below. Roll two dice to select two items at random. For example if you roll a 2 followed by a 4 – the word is circle. Repeat to find the second word. How might they be put together and what could that combined image symbolise?

	1	2	3	4	5	6
1	Sword	Flame	Flower	Door	Fish	Shield
2	Sky	Leaf	Pathway	Wheat	Crown	Boat
3	Mountain	Moon	Book	Globe	Heart	Fish
4	Lamp	Circle	Pen	Pennant	Castle	Cauldron
5	Bridge	Jewel	Lion	River	Horizon	Fruit
6	Bird	Sun	Ladder	Torch	Feather	Wagon

Prayer Flags and 'Spiritual Collage'

Key ideas:

Expressing deeply held thoughts and feelings through simple acts of making. Creative expression is a bridge to heightened spiritual awareness.

The use of prayer flags has been part of the spiritual tradition of China, Tibet, Persia and India for hundreds of years. Prayers, symbols, mantras and messages of peace are printed on pieces of coloured cloth. These are then strung between poles and allowed to blow in the wind, which is said to carry 'beneficent vibrations' across the land. Prayer flags are thought to bring happiness, long life and prosperity to the flag planter and those in the vicinity. An Internet search will immediately supply you with plenty of images and further information.

Making prayer flags with the children is a memorable way of helping them to understand the qualities of a spiritually intelligent person – integrity, compassion, self-respect, regard for others, appreciation of the world we live in, empathy, courage, selflessness and so on. The activity creates the opportunity to express and represent these and other feelings, and to be reminded of the words of wisdom that have come down to us through the centuries from all over the world.

Let me emphasise that while prayer flags have long been a part of (Buddhist) religious tradition, having the children create them does not need to be a religious activity in itself. The word prayer itself means 'obtained by entreaty', which in a religious context means obtained by entreaty to God, but has equal value as an entreaty by one human being to another.

To do:

As well as making flags, you might consider these other related activities:

■ A spiritual collage. Invite the children each to draw a picture or symbol which is meaningful to them in becoming more spiritually aware. Arrange these on a display board as a collage.

■ Message to the world. Children choose a quote or create their own message on a cardboard tag. Attach these to helium balloons and let the wind take them where it will.

■ Peace Post-its. Suggest that children write their messages of peace on a sticky note. Create a central place in the school where they can be displayed.

■ Treasure box. The word 'shrine' originally meant a case or a box for keeping precious papers, usually showing reverence for a deity, ancestor, hero, saint or other highly respected person. Since I believe we all need heroes, have the children pack small boxes dedicated to certain people they admire and respect. Such boxes might contain pictures, articles, letters (posted or not!) and quotes from the person concerned. Children can be invited to make presentations to the rest of the group about their chosen hero.

Spirituality means taking a moment to appreciate all the good things in our lives; our homes, families and friends, a beautiful sunrise or a tree swaying in the wind, and saying thank you to the universe for all these wonderful things. It is about looking beyond the mundane. And without it the world would seem one-dimensional.

Lors

Sound Bath

Key idea:

To have the experience of going on a journey through engagement with the sense of sound.

To do:

■ Invite the group to think of sounds that would symbolise a calm place. The sounds need to be ones they can make with their voices or by tapping their bodies, clapping their hands or moving their feet. They might choose to make the sound of the wind blowing calmly, of birds singing, waves lapping and so on.

■ Talk about what sort of places make us feel calm, and what sort of sounds relax us.

■ When everyone in the group has a sound, invite them to share these individually. This will give you an idea of your musical palate. If two or more sounds pupils make are the same you might choose to place those people close together to give that sound more volume.

■ Once you have heard everyone ask the group if there are other sounds that could be made that would enhance the atmosphere you are trying to create. If anyone feels there are sounds missing, ask who would like to be responsible for these. (Sometimes it is easier to make two or three pupils responsible for one sound.)

■ Listen to the sounds again individually to remind you of your palate. Then as a conductor begin to create a soundscape, bringing in the different sounds, raising the volume of certain sounds, inviting some sounds to repeat or keep going and others to come in briefly. Use your hands to indicate turning up and down of volume or to invite other pupils in.

■ Once you have fine-tuned your sounds, invite three to five children to sit on the floor in the middle of the room. Invite the rest of the group to stand around them in a tight circle. The pupils in the middle must close their eyes while the pupils around the outside send their sounds down into the ground towards the children that are sitting there. You can still conduct or depending on the group you can invite them to improvise their sounds, coming in and out at various times to create an atmosphere.

■ After a few minutes indicate for the group to become silent, hold the silence for a few beats then invite the pupils in the middle of the circle to open their eyes and talk about what they experienced, or the story of their journey when their eyes were shut.

■ The experience of a sound bath is incredibly powerful and can be used to explore all kinds of atmospheres or environments. Creating a calming environment can give participants a sense of peace or create images of amazing landscapes in the brain. Being bathed in sound by others in your group creates a kaleidoscope for the senses and most participants open their eyes from it in a heightened state, similar to that achieved through meditation. Allowing pupils to share their stories and thoughts after this experience is important and can give you new insights into your students.

Take it further:

■ The same technique can be used to create the sounds of a storm at sea, or a forest at night. Experiment with different atmospheres, calming or dramatic.

■ Explore painting pictures in the mind using sound and sound baths. Invite groups of pupils to rehearse creating an environment using only sound. Then allow the group to sound bath three to five pupils, in a circle around them and sending the sound down towards the ground. Invite the rest of the class to close their eyes as well while the sounds are made. At the end of the exercise ask the pupils who experienced the sound bath to talk about their experience. Did the rest of the class have a similar experience, bearing in mind that they were not hearing the sound in such an intense fashion?

A walk in the woods to me is all a visit to a church should be, as well as the counsel of my elders – the trees, the restorative nature of smelling damp leaves and hearing the silence of a million bugs and insects at their tasks brings me a certainty and solace I have not found elsewhere.

Tab Neal

Self-Expression

Stories

This Is Me!

Key ideas:

We are sometimes so keen to show how different, talented or unique we are that we forget that there are talents we have that have yet to be discovered. Parents are key to the development (or suppression) of all our talents and to focus too soon on one talent can block the road to other joys.

Thomas was 7 years old and what some people would call a gifted or talented child. Thomas's parents David and Susan, who'd had very little in the way of luxuries as children, wanted to give Thomas everything in life to make him happy. And they did. Because they loved him. They had planned – when Thomas was grown up, independent and could live without them – that they would travel the world. They both loved travelling but took their parental responsibilities very seriously and had therefore agreed to forgo any international exploration until Thomas was 18. But first they wanted to give Thomas everything that he wanted so that he could grow into a happy adult and make his way in the world.

Thomas had his own room (the biggest room in the house because his parents wanted him to have it). In the room he had everything that money could buy: a computer (and all the latest games), a huge TV with surround-sound and the latest clothes including trainers and jeans and very expensive designer T-shirts. Thomas had only to ask for something and he would get it because his parents loved him.

It was Thomas's seventh birthday and he had his friends over for a party. They had games and food and Thomas had loads of presents. Thomas was very happy.

When all the other children had gone and Thomas was playing with his new games his parents said there was a special gift from them to him. They asked him to close his eyes whilst they led him to his big surprise. Thomas did not want to close his eyes because he was scared of the dark so his parents said he could keep his eyes open.

'Remember that picture you did of yourself last month?' asked his mother. 'Well Daddy and I were so impressed we thought you deserved a studio of your own.'

They took Thomas to one of the spare rooms (they had a large house) and opened the door. Inside was everything that an artist would need. There were paints and brushes, an easel, paper, crayons, charcoal … everything.

Thomas was delighted. Yes, he remembered the picture he had drawn that he was so delighted with. It was a self-portrait.

The balloon shaped face with stern looking eyes and an irritated down-turned line for a mouth was not an exact mirror image of Thomas but it did resemble him. It captured his mood.

'This is brilliant, you're a real artist,' his Dad said. 'Are you going to be an artist when you grow up? You could you know, with talent like this, what's to stop you?'

'I could sell my paintings and buy a big house, couldn't I Dad?'

'Absolutely, you are an artistic genius.'

Thomas realised that he was an artist (his parents had made him a studio so he must be). The next day he asked his Dad for an old shirt as he had seen a picture of a real artist in a smock and wanted to look the part. He took out a big sheet of paper and set about drawing himself again (he was good at this).

After a while there was a telephone call from Thomas's best friend James who wanted to know if Thomas wanted to come round and play. James's mother was an excellent gardener and cook and was going to show Thomas how to make an apple pie with real apples from the garden. Thomas said no. He was an artist and that is all he wanted to do. So James invited Ryan, who was his second best friend, but who would soon become James's first best friend.

That evening Thomas was getting ready for bed and his mother came in with a storybook all about a bear that had some interesting and strange friends who went on many adventures, but Thomas was not interested. He only wanted to look at books about artists and how to draw or paint. So Thomas's mother put the books about bears and other things away and went and got the book about artists. The next day she boxed up all the books that Thomas did not want to look at and bought some new books about art (particularly how to draw yourself). She loved Thomas and wanted to give him everything he wanted.

The next day his father was doing his accounts and asked Thomas to come and help him tap some numbers into a calculator (a job he usually loved).

'Sorry Dad, I am an artist and artists do not do numbers – they do drawing and painting.' And with that Thomas went back to his room and began drawing another picture of himself that was going to be even better than the last one.

Over the coming days and weeks Thomas refused to spend time with friends who wanted him to go swimming (I am an artist and artists do not do sport!); or sing songs (I am an artist and artists do not do music!); or read and make up stories (I am an artist and artists do not need words, they need pictures). Thomas only wanted to do pictures (of himself) and did not want to waste his talents on playing games and doing things with other people.

One day a few weeks after Thomas realised that he was an artist he told his parents that he did not want to go to school as he had everything that he needed to be an artist at home.

His parents loved him very much and did not want to upset him and so they called the school and said that Thomas would not be coming back to school as he was an artist now, and so Maths, English, sport, music, gardening and working with other children was a waste of his time.

The teacher tried to explain to Thomas's parents that Thomas would need to have skills in all the subjects so that when he left school he would have greater choice in what he did for a job.

But Thomas's parents loved him so much they did not want to upset him and thanked the teacher for her concern but Thomas would not be returning to school, ever.

Eleven years later Thomas was still at home with his parents painting pictures and doing drawings of himself. And they were very good. They may even have been the best pictures of a young man alone in a room without friends or interests other than completing self-portraits that have ever been, or will ever be, produced.

But today is Thomas's eighteenth birthday and his parents have given Thomas his presents (art materials and a very fine wooden easel). They have also left a note for Thomas on his breakfast tray that they had placed outside his room (Thomas now took all of his meals in his room, alone).

This is what was written in the letter to Thomas:

Dear Thomas,

We hope that we have been good parents and have tried to give you everything that you wanted so that you could grow up and have a happy life. Well, now that you are 18 you are officially an adult and so we are going to leave you as we would like to travel and see the world before we get too old.

We will be gone for about five years but will send you postcards and call you now and again to let you know how we are.

Please look after the house and here is a list of the things that you absolutely have to do to keep alive.

Get a job and make some money and make sure you earn more than you spend otherwise life will be hard. Look after the garden. There are lots of fruit and vegetables growing there but you do need to plant and feed and grow and store and cook them.

You might want to improve your reading and writing as there are lots of forms that you will have to sign if you want to have a bank account or buy a car. As you do not have a car you will have to take a bus or walk. We know that you have not left the house for eleven years but you might need to. We have left granddad's old bicycle in the garage but it is a bit heavy and does require quite a lot of physical effort to get it going.

We have also left cousin Steven's old guitar (remember, he gave you this when you were 9 years old but you never even took it out of the case). This will be a nice way to spend your time and could also help you make some money and is a good way of meeting new people.

People. Well, Thomas, you have not seen anyone but us for eleven years, and you have barely spoken to us in this time, but you might have to come out of your room and work with other people. Of all the many different and special gifts that people have from art or music, gardening or maths, writing, thinking or sport, if you are not able to listen to and talk with other people then life will be very tough and lonely. Without being able to play, work or even have a passing interest in the needs and feelings of others you might as well stay in your room and never come out.

See you in five years,

Love

Mum and Dad xx

Thomas read the letter and thought for a while. He then left the tray and the letter outside his room and closed the door.

Thomas's parents loved him. They loved him to death.

To do:

Ask the children to do a self-portrait and to draw objects or images of things that interest them. They then present themselves to the rest of the class or group. Encourage the children to ask questions about each others' interests.

Take it further:

List Howard Gardner's multiple intelligences as different ways of being smart: word smart, number smart, self smart, picture smart, music smart, body smart, nature smart, people smart. You can present these in words and/or pictures and use this as a basis for discussion.

Key questions:

Do we need some intelligences or ways of being smart more than others? Which intelligence is the most important in life? Can you become smart in an area that you may not be smart in at the moment? If so, how? What stopped Thomas from developing all of his skills?

Spirituality – it's a place, somewhere you find yourself. It is a moment you find yourself in, something combines with you and that moment to produce it. It can also be a set of circumstances, occur through a challenge or a harsh circumstance, like a flat tyre, standing beside the road as the motorway whizzes past, and suddenly your urgent appointment can't be and everything has had to stop. It can be upon you in an instant and stay for hours or be very fleeting. It's there for a reason, to lift us up, to lift us above and to make sense and to motivate us, recharge us, help us face another day.

Paul Lyalls

Divine Inspiration

Key ideas:

There are different ways of expressing ourselves. And we've all had times when we've wished we could do something as well as other people – be it playing sport in a team or being in a band. But where do these gifts come from? In the Christian tradition there are many stories of 'divine inspiration'.

Cædmon

In 661, an Anglo Saxon monk called Bede lived in a monastery at Jarrow, on the banks of the River Tyne in the north-east of England. He wrote a long book called *The Ecclesiastical History of the English People* and in it he told a story about a man called Cædmon.

Cædmon was a monk at the monastery of Whitby Abbey. As was the tradition after the meal, the harp was passed around. But Cædmon couldn't sing and usually when he was at a feast he would slip out. But one night, as he slept in the barn, he had a dream. He dreamt that someone came to him and said, 'Cædmon, sing to me about the beginning of the world.'

'No,' replied Cædmon, 'I cannot sing, and I can't play the harp.' But then he tried really hard, and made up some lines about how God created the world.

The next morning Cædmon woke up and remembered his dream. He told his poem to the abbess, who said, 'Truly this is a gift from God.'

Cædmon went on to became a monk who was famous for turning bible teachings into beautiful poems and songs.

This is a translation of his *Hymn*:

Now we shall praise the place that is heaven

The might of the Maker, the thoughts of his mind

The father of splendour who set out these wonders

The Lord Everlasting, the early creator.

The first thing he shaped for the children of old

Was the roof we call heaven, the Holy one made

Middle Earth for us next, he was mankind's protector

The Lord Everlasting who finally fashioned

A place for his people, Praise the Almighty.

Translated by Tim Harding

To do:

- ■ Cædmon had the gift of writing poetry and songs, expressing his feelings in words. Use his example as a starting point for discussion about individual/personal gifts. You could use the following questions to help structure the responses: Do you feel that you have a gift? Is there something you're good at? Why do you think you are good at this thing? Where has your ability to be good at this come from? Is it something you have inherited from your family? Is it something you have been taught or have practised?

- ■ Expand the discussion by asking: How do you use this talent?

- ■ You could also explore the possibility that a talent or gift may not always be used to good purpose.

Take it further:

Cædmon felt useless compared to the other men who could sing and play the harp. But then through his 'dream' he realised that he could be just as good, if he used his gifts in God's service as a monk. Discuss the idea of a God – a supreme being who intervenes on a personal level to shape people's lives. This is what Cædmon believed had happened to him and this is one of the cornerstones of Christian belief.

Spirituality comes out in me as a strong feeling of wanting to do something positive, to make a real difference in life, to change the world and tackle social injustice – my spirituality guides me in what feels right and what feels wrong.

Matt

Do Your Own Thing

Key ideas:

Our lives are a balance of structured tasks and opportunities to be creative. Structured routines can give us the security and confidence to express ourselves.

A few years ago I used to play the trombone in a jazz band. Trad jazz they called it. There were three 'lead' instruments: Andy the trumpet player always played the tune, Gill the clarinettist played at double speed around the tune, and I played a harmony part on the trombone, filling in the gaps. There was also a rhythm section: Karl on drums kept the rhythm and Jo and Sam played the chords on bass and piano. Sometimes we had music to play from, but other times we just played an arrangement of a song we all knew, and we organised it like this.

We all played along with the tune.

Then the trumpeter would play a solo, based on the tune, but with his own made-up ideas in it.

The rhythm section would still be playing along, keeping the time and playing chords to keep the 'shape' of the piece.

Then we'd all play along with the tune again.

Then the clarinettist would solo.

Then we'd all play the tune again.

Then it was my solo.

Then we'd all play the tune again a couple of times to finish off.

You always had the chance to come back to the tune that you were familiar with. It was great. In the solos you could show how good you were – or not (I'm not the world's greatest trombonist!).

But all the time you had the rhythm section playing the chords along with you so you knew where things were going – and you knew when to go back to the tune – the 'head' as jazz players sometimes call it.

It's also how groups of people have been playing for hundreds of years. Elizabethan lute players used to do the same thing – taking turns to 'improvise' around a well known tune.

To do:

■ Set up a musical improvisation experience at an appropriate level for the skills of your group. It could be as simple as clapping rhythm patterns. Alternate between all playing the same thing and then giving individuals the opportunity to make their own rhythms while the rest keep the beat.

■ Ask the children whether they prefer playing along with everyone else or taking a solo. What would happen if the rhythm section all started doing their own thing at the same time?

Take it further:

Ask the pupils how they like to express themselves. Is it through dance, drawing, writing words or some other way? Do they need structures for these activities or are they happy to go it alone?

> *I have always struggled with any concept of God, especially the idea of an old man on a cloud and I never understood why there weren't dinosaurs in the Garden of Eden. I've sat in beautiful churches, respecting the faith that built them, waiting patiently for the bolt of lightning and for a sign. It never came. But I've been looking in the wrong places. The energy for good and light is within us, within our strength, our hope, our creativity and our faith. It is in our ability to communicate with and love each other, in our ability to survive a crisis with dignity and humility.*
>
> **Jules**

New Year's Eve

Key idea:

Exploring a fresh start.

New Year can be a time for a strong sense of spiritual connectedness to the world.

My mum's birthday is on New Year's Day, so as a child New Year's Eve took on an extra significance. I remember it as a time of being allowed to stay up and wait for the magical moment when we finished with the old and brought in the new.

As the hours towards midnight ticked by we would watch television, or tell stories, make New Year's resolutions, or fidget restlessly, killing time and constantly watching the clock till that special moment arrived.

And then in tune with the whole of the UK and alongside whichever presenter was running the BBC's New Year's Eve celebrations, my mother, my sister and I would stand up and in a loud voice begin the countdown: 10, 9, 8, 7, 6, 5, 4, 3, 2, 1.

As Big Ben chimed, all three of us would cheer and clap, alone in our front room but connected with the world.

Following shouts of 'Happy New Year' and 'Happy Birthday', we would cross our arms and hold hands in the smallest of circles necessitated by our family of three, and accompanying Scotland we would dance and sing the famous 'Auld Lang Syne'.

Then the final part of the ritual began: the ringing of bells, ridding the house of all the bad spirits from the previous year and ringing in the new.

Our three small brass bells were clutched eagerly in our hands as we ran around the house clanging them as loudly as their tiny sounds could go, chiming new energy into our home.

Then with New Year and birthday greetings buzzing on our lips we would climb the stairs to bed, contented in the belief of new possibilities and hope.

As I grew older and left home the importance of New Year's Eve stayed with me. At parties you can guarantee that as midnight arrives I am the one who grabs the hands of anyone close to me, and stunned by my friends' lack of knowledge of the words, I still lead a very rowdy and out of tune chorus of 'Auld Lang Syne'.

As for New Year's resolutions, I don't do these anymore. My sister had a brilliant idea that rather than thinking of New Year as a time to give things up, why not spend some time on New Year's Eve contemplating the things you hope to achieve in the coming year.

So now on New Year's Eve we sit and make collages of the things we would like to achieve, places we would like to visit and hopes and dreams for the coming year. The pictures serve as a reminder of the wishes we had on that special evening where everything felt possible. The things we achieve from this list we smile about, and as for the things we don't achieve, well they obviously weren't as important as we first thought.

So for me, New Year's Eve is a time of connectedness with the universe, a time of change. It is a time to move on from the mistakes of the previous year and to embrace the possibilities of the year ahead. It is as if the whole universe holds its breath at midnight, slates are wiped clean, and we can enter the New Year on a fresh page.

To do:

- Invite your class to create a collage of things they want to achieve in the coming year. This does not have to be a New Year's Eve activity. It could be at the start of a new term or a new academic year.

- Discuss how different times of the year make you feel. What rituals or celebrations do you have to mark these times?

- What does making a fresh start mean to pupils in your class? Are there certain times in the year or in your life when it feels more possible to make a fresh start?

Once Upon a Time There Was a Girl

Once upon a time there was a girl and the girl was very married. And she danced to the music with her marries. And then there was a big bad wolf sneaking while she was dancing. And then they looked behind them and then they saw a wolf. And the wolf gobbled them up. And then they was alive again. And then they went home and then they saw a broken chair. So much the liked the broken chair that it broked into little pieces. And they then sitted on their new settee.

Story by Bethany, aged 4

Illustration by Hanif, aged 6

Activities

Natural Curiosity

Key ideas:

The importance of curiosity and humour in developing spiritual awareness. Developing children's questioning techniques.

During one school visit I made I was being shown to the library to talk to a class. The librarian was taking me the 'indoor way', which was reserved for staff and guests (students had to take a longer outdoor route). But one child certainly had been through there recently because stuck to a noticeboard was a piece of paper featuring a drawing of Mr Chad and this instruction on a tab of paper: 'Do Not Lift!'

'Look at that,' I said. My host was annoyed and embarrassed. 'Oh, I'm sorry about that defacement.' 'No, I mean have you ever lifted the tab?' 'Certainly not!' was the reply. 'I've got to lift it, I've got to know...' And because I was a guest I was allowed to – and was delighted to read when I did so: 'Nosy Parker!' (or words to that effect).

For me this is a perfect illustration of the attitude that not only drives all human endeavour but is vital in raising spiritual awareness. And I don't just mean the urge to lift the tab, but also the mischievous sense of humour of the person who set up the joke. I assumed it was a child, but would be pleased to learn it was one of the staff.

Although we are all born with the gift of natural curiosity it often fades from children's lives for any number of reasons. But as educationalists we can cultivate and encourage it in simple but effective ways.

To do:

◼ Allow questioning to become the heart of your lessons – if not every time then on a regular basis.

◼ Set some ground rules for the children's questioning behaviour:

◆ All children have the right to ask questions without fear of judgement or ridicule.

◆ Ideally questions should be about what the children find interesting and relevant.

◆ Criteria of quality for questions are that they should be relevant, appropriate and substantive.

◆ The best questions to ask are those that you don't know the answers to (but how might we find out?).

◆ Often the most powerful questions have a number of answers (or no answers at all as far as we know).

■ Encourage open questioning that stimulates divergent thinking. Value 'contingent thinking' where children can feel safe to say, 'Well, it depends...'

■ Make the 'Six Big Important Questions' high profile in the classroom: who, what, where, when, why and how. Take every opportunity to allow such questioning across the subject range.

Take it further:

■ Consider introducing philosophical enquiry as an element of the learning environment.

■ Constantly emphasise that asking questions is not a sign of ignorance or stupidity: in fact it is intelligent behaviour that means 'I'm keen to find out more'.

■ Help children to understand that 'answers' are not just matters of fact. Feelings, intuitions, hunches, inklings and other types of 'inner knowing' become valid in areas such as spirituality.

■ Cultivate respect for children's answers. Encourage 'I think this because...' behaviour.

Playing with Words

Key ideas:

Words can communicate and stir up powerful images and feelings. Words only refer to things and are not those things themselves. Greater awareness of the effect words can have on us gives us greater self-control and makes us more powerful.

The scientist and philosopher Alfred Korzybski sagely pointed out that 'the word is not the thing'. This idea has also been framed as 'the map is not the territory' and 'the menu is not the meal'. While most adults understand that language is merely representational, in our everyday lives we often allow ourselves to be influenced by words – by what the writer Alan Watts has called 'those little puffs of air'. The old proverb tells us that sticks and stones may break my bones, but names can never hurt me. What nonsense that is in so many ways! How wonderful it would be if it were true.

I remember running a creative writing workshop in a school one time. As the children wrote I heard the class teacher say to one boy, 'Well I was hoping for something better from you.' Now I suppose you could take that as an indication of the teacher's high expectations for that pupil, but the child didn't. He looked hurt and angry and refused to commit himself to paper any more. (The word 'commit' by the way has associations that could put anybody off trying to write!) I thought to myself that those few words and the negative feelings they evoked might stay with that boy for years. What terrible damage they may have done.

One aspect of raising spiritual awareness is appreciating how the world looks from other people's viewpoints. This develops empathy and is a creative act insofar as it encourages multiple perspectives – looking at the world through many windows.

To do:

Another aspect is to notice how words influence and (another creative act) to go beyond them; to see them for what they are, little puffs of air, a convenient shorthand. Activities that have worked well for me in this regard include:

■ Inventing new words and definitions. A Year 6 class recently came up with:

◆ an experi-meant-well – a scientist who tries hard but keeps getting it wrong.

◆ scuttering – a cross between scuttling and scattering.

◆ slanger – slow anger, a simmering rage and/or bearing a grudge.

◆ remember – allowing someone to join a group all over again (read it re-member).

■ Making up new proverbs or reworking old ones. How might we reframe this proverb: 'Four things come not back: the spoken word, the sped arrow, the past life and the neglected opportunity'?

■ Exploring word origins. Etymology throws up some fascinating insights. Check out: inspiration, enthusiasm, measure, fact, religion, holy, homage, text.

The Flower Is Red and the Willow Is Green

Key ideas:

The importance of making up one's own mind. Exploring the connections between independence of judgement and developing spiritual awareness.

An ancient piece of Zen wisdom advises us that the flower is red and the willow is green. Immediately afterwards another piece of Zen wisdom declares with equal authority that the flower is not red and the willow is not green. This is typical of the simple clarity yet sometimes infuriating subtlety of Zen, which often delivers aphorisms like these with a childlike and mischievous humour – an important quality, incidentally, in the development of spiritual intelligence.

The flower-is-red-is-not-red conundrum encapsulates a number of important ideas in helping children to become more spiritually aware:

■ The word is not the thing. And, whatever we say something is, it is not; which is to say that language is only ever a shorthand approximation of what we think and perceive. The idea can be explored for instance by handing out small objects like stones, leaves or shells and asking the children to describe them. This can only be done to a certain extent, after which we realise that an incredible number of small details make up even a simple object. Beyond a certain point language fails us – or it's too much effort to keep using it!

■ *Vive la différence!* The world is infinitely varied. By noticing, for example, how many reds and greens there are in a garden or classroom refines the senses, challenges our descriptive abilities and enhances our appreciation of the world's richness.

■ One's own direct experiences are vital in developing spirituality. It's easy to be led by authority and swayed by dogma. If I am told by an expert, and assertively enough, that the flower is red and the willow is green I might believe it unquestioningly. Read *The Emperor's New Clothes* with the children and invite them to make up similar stories that explore the same idea.

■ It's OK not to know the right answers right now. It's also fine to say 'I don't know' and 'I don't understand'. In fact these are two of the 'assertive rights' listed by Manuel J. Smith in his book *When I Say No, I Feel Guilty*. This ethos can be developed in children through philosophical enquiry (see Stephen Bowkett and Sara Stanley's *But Why?* and Stephen Law's *The Philosophy Files 1* and *2*).

■ An appreciation of something need not be put into words at all. It was St Augustine who said, 'I know what time is until you ask me to define it.' This is related to the idea of explaining colour to a blind person. Encourage children to appreciate things – music, scented oils, artwork and so on – without any need or pressure to describe, analyse or put into words. As another piece of Zen wisdom tells us, how do you help someone to understand the idea of saltiness? Just let him taste salt.

To do:

■ All of the above ideas offer themes for discussion with the class.

■ What are some of the things in our lives that we can't easily put into words?

■ How else can we express those things?

■ Why do we sometimes (often?) believe what we are told?

■ With big questions to do with what the universe means and our purpose in life, how can we begin to find answers?

'Myku'

Key ideas:

Big ideas can be expressed in simple ways. Important insights can be found everywhere.

'Myku' is a recently invented term meaning 'my haiku'. Haiku is a poetical form that developed in ancient Japan and was brought to a peak of elegance and quiet power by the poet Matsuo Kinsaku (1644–94), who changed his name to Basho in honour of the gift of a basho tree presented to him by a disciple. By the time Basho appeared on the scene the haiku was, according to the poet and translator Lucian Stryk, 'expiring of artificiality' because of the huge number of rigid rules imposed on the form by what Stryk calls 'the rule-smiths'. Basho's great contribution was to bend and even discard rules thus allowing poetic expression to arise organically and naturally out of his own life experience.

Although many children learn about haiku in primary school, fewer I think understand the connection between such poetry and spirituality. Basho's haiku came to articulate his realisation of deeply held truths about existence within the Zen tradition that he embraced or which, one might say, came to embrace him. His work again and again connects simple observations of the natural world and of everyday events with what he saw as the essential unity and wonder of all life. And in line with the way of Zen, a small mundane detail often serves to reveal something of the sacred, suggesting an answer to the most profound and soul-searching of questions.

To do:

■ Explain how myku are a simpler form of the haiku poem (if children haven't studied haiku, use myku as an introduction). Show them the examples below.

■ Ask children to pick a theme and create some myku.

■ Now ask them to make myku about the biggest, deepest questions they ever think about – Why am I here? Is there a God? Why do so many people believe (or disbelieve) in a deity?

The 'standard' haiku poem consists of three lines with a syllable structure of 5-7-5. The myku form is simpler – 2-3-4 syllables across three lines. This means that children have to choose words carefully and keep things simple, which includes chopping out any unnecessary words. When I ask children to try writing myku I tell them that the poem is often about noticing some small detail and how that can lead to a sudden understanding (i.e. Look I notice this – Wow I realise *this*!). The use of a dash can mark the moment of realisation…

> *Petals*
> *blowing free –*
> *they tell it all.*

> *Kitten*
> *lives then dies –*
> *the world's story.*

> *Daisies*
> *on waste ground –*
> *Always themselves!*

Myku need not – I think should not – be confined to 'Literacy', but can be written within any subject about any topic. One Year 5 child recently penned this as our class conversation came round to the fortieth anniversary of the first moon landing:

> *Moonlight*
> *still so cool*
> *despite big boots!*

I'm sure you'll appreciate what a great opportunity for discussion and debate is bundled up here in this simple, humorous and very insightful piece of writing.

Another value of myku poetry is that it acts as a stepping-stone to the more sophisticated haiku form. Josh, who wrote the myku above, worked on it further and came up with:

Moonlight, wonderful
despite touch of spacecraft fire,
rocks brought home in bags.

He really wanted to put '*and* rocks brought home in bags'. We talked about rules and how Basho was their master rather than their slave and, in the end, he put the additional word in that final line.

A Moon on Water

Key idea:

Exploring spiritual ideas through metaphor.

In the Zen tradition there is a saying that becoming spiritually aware is like a moon reflected on water: the *moon does not get wet*, nor is the water broken. Now you may wish to ponder this idea (as I have for years), but you can also use it to help children explore metaphor in a creative way.

To do:

■ Show the class a picture of a moon reflected on water and invite them to make statements (spoken or written) about what they notice and what they are reminded of. Suggestions from a Year 6 class include:

◆ It's two moons but one moon at the same time.

◆ Which is the real moon?

◆ If there were ten puddles there'd be eleven moons.

◆ If there were a million puddles there'd be a million and one moons!

◆ The moon adds to the water and the water adds to the moon.

◆ Look, a moon on the ground! How surprising!

◆ I can put my face right beside the moon – both reflected in the water.

◆ The moon shivers with the slightest breath of wind.

◆ The moon reflects the sunlight. The puddle reflects the moonlight. I'm looking at sunlight in the night-time!

Take it further:

Apart from the children inadvertently creating some beautiful imagery and profound metaphors, with a little juggling (of the metaphors not the children) you can make the most delicate and memorable poetry (shaping them into haiku if you wish, or 'myku' – see page 119).

Water,
dead of night –
reflected moon!

A moon
on the ground –
How surprising!

Here, there
two moons glow –
Which one is real?

Extend the activity by asking children to let some of their statements represent much bigger ideas, such as:

■ *The moon adds to the water and the water adds to the moon.* If this said something useful about how to live a happy life, what do you learn?

■ *Look a moon on the ground. How surprising?* How could we use this idea to cut down on global pollution?

■ *The moon shivers with the slightest breath of wind.* How can this idea help a lonely person to make more friends?

Finally, there are some excellent collections of Japanese folk sayings that can add variety to the activities suggested above (e.g. Shigematsu's *A Zen Harvest*). Use the sayings as they appear or abstract the essential image or idea for the children to work on:

■ I watch my step but slip on the snowy path.

■ I am like a wind chime. Whether I ring or not depends on the breeze.

■ The blowing leaf shows its face for a second and then turns away.

■ No matter how wise I become the willow is no greener than before.

■ The sea rolls and swells all day long.

■ Here's an answer – the sound of the wind drawn in ink on a white sheet of paper.

Screen Savers

Key idea:

Sometimes visual images can help us to focus on the things that are important to us, and also to express what spirituality is to us.

What's on your screen saver? Maybe you've got pictures of yourself or of people or places that are special to you. What does your screensaver say about you? My computer screen-saver is a picture of a place I often visit – it's a special place for me: the Farne Islands in my home county of Northumberland.

I find inspiration in the power of the sea, the distance of the horizon and the wildness of it all. As I look at the picture I can imagine the feel of the boat riding the swell, the sound of the seagulls, the wonder of the seals poking their heads out of the water to watch us as we pass by. During the seventh century, the Farne Islands were inhabited by the Celtic Christian monk Cuthbert who found peace and solitude amongst the sea birds. People would visit him there. It may be that the name Farne Islands means 'Islands of the Travellers'. Nowadays when you visit the islands, you can still sense the timeless peace and solitude that many people over the centuries travelled there to experience.

My screensaver provides a calming start to my day when I fire up my computer, reminding me of past experiences. So too other screensavers can provoke reactions – some make us smile, some remind us of friends, some inspire – we can choose. And we can choose the depth to which we are drawn in – a quick glance or a deeper reflection. Just as we can choose the depth of our own spirituality.

To do:

■ Ask the pupils: Have you got a special picture? Can you describe it in words? What does it mean to you? Does it bring back memories of a person or event? If it is a place have you been there? What can you remember about being there?

■ Find a picture of a person and get the children to look beyond the physical aspects of the portrait to explore the emotions behind the picture. They could express their responses in poetry or perhaps a song.

Take it further:

Ask the pupils to design a class computer screensaver – each pupil can contribute to a montage with images of special significance, either to individuals or the group. The screensavers could be changed on a regular basis, perhaps reflecting festivals or seasons which have a particular significance to the pupils.

Building a Shed

Key idea:

Self-expression also has an impact on others and if we are to celebrate our own individuality in an open and healthy way then we need to be able to recognise the impact that our words and actions have on others.

To do:

■ Invite the class to stand in a circle. Next teach them the following two-person dialogue:

Person 1:   What are you doing?

Person 2:   I'm building a shed.

Person 1:   Can I join in?

Person 2:   Of course you can.

■ Once the class have learnt the dialogue, ask one person to go into the middle of the circle and start miming the action that would demonstrate building a shed.

■ Then ask another person to enter the circle and begin the dialogue as Person 1. The person already in the middle replies in role as Person 2, and as soon as they say, 'of course you can,' Person 1 starts miming another action towards building the shed.

■ Next invite someone else to come into the circle and begin the dialogue as Person 1, but this time they should do it as if they are crying. This time both people who are building the shed reply in unison, using the lines 'We're building a shed.' The difference this time is that they have to mirror the emotion of Person 1, so the dialogue is said in a tearful manner. As soon as the two people in the mirror say 'of course you can' all three people continue to mime different aspects of building the shed tearfully.

■ The fourth person arrives happily, and immediately their joy is infectious. The dialogue repeats with the three people in the circle speaking happily in unison about what they are doing and the new arrival smiling as they eventually join in with the building.

■ Take it in turns to send in more people with differing emotions. The fifth person could be angry, the sixth person could be shy, the seventh scared and the eighth bored.

■ As you feed in more people notice how the different emotions affect the players. The ninth player could be laughing, the tenth could be confused, the eleventh is calm and the twelfth could be ecstatic.

■ Keep involving more people in the activity, suggesting differing emotions to the group and allowing them to explore what each new sentiment does to the now familiar dialogue.

■ Stop the activity when you feel like you have enough people building the shed. And use the exercise to begin a discussion about emotions, and the affect of emotions on us all.

■ Ask the group who performed if they found that different emotions affected the way they worked on the shed. How do one person's emotions affect the people around them?

■ Did the group who were watching see anything different? Are some emotions easier to relate to than others? Did they create any stories to explain the emotions of each new person coming in?

This exercise is a great way to lead into discussion about different types of emotions and what makes us feel happy, sad, angry and so on. And also how do our emotions affect others?

Giving and Receiving

Key idea:

To explore the emotions connected with giving and receiving.

To do:

■ In a circle, one at a time, mime giving a gift to the person next to you. Imagine the box that the gift comes in and think about the weight and the size of the gift. Place the gift in front of the person you are giving it to. They have to open the box, reach inside and take out something and mime using it.

■ The person who has received the gift then has to express extreme gratitude to their partner. Telling them why they have always wanted such a gift and how it is the best thing they have ever received. The giver of the gift can only smile while the praise for their generosity is given.

■ The person who has received the gift has to then give a different gift to the next person in the circle and so the exercise continues until everyone has either given or received a gift.

Discussion:

How did it feel giving a gift and being praised so heavily for it? Is it better to give or receive a gift? Which one do you prefer? What does it feel like if you are given a gift that you really don't like?

Take it further:

■ Invite one person to stand in the middle of the circle. Tell your class that as soon as this person arrives at the middle they all have to start clapping and cheering and whooping like they have never seen anyone do something so amazing before in their lives. The person in the middle needs to stand and smile and accept the praise.

■ Give other pupils a turn to experience this. Each time the class has to respond as if they have never seen anything so brilliant before in their lives.

■ After several pupils have had a go, invite them to share with the class what it felt like to receive so much positive praise and clapping and cheering.

■ How did it feel for the rest of the class to clap and cheer so enthusiastically?

■ Is it hard to receive praise? Do you prefer giving or receiving? Which is the easiest? Why?

A Secret Place

Key idea:

To appreciate the need for your own space, to create an environment where you can contemplate the world.

To do:

■ Invite your students to imagine a place where they can go that no one knows about; a place where they can sit on their own with just their thoughts and escape from everyone else, a secret place.

■ Give out the worksheets and invite students to draw or write a description of this place. Encourage them to imagine where it is. What can they hear when they sit in their secret place? Perhaps it is a garden and they can hear birdsong, or maybe it is a cave and the sound that accompanies their thoughts are the waves crashing below.

■ Once students have begun to visualise their ideas about this secret place get them into pairs and invite them to share with their partner their secret world. This should be enacted, with pupils talking and walking their partner through the journey, climbing over rocks, moving carefully on the slippery moss steps, ducking down so that your head doesn't get knocked on the overhanging tree. Once they have arrived, ask them to sit together in the secret place and imagine they are looking at all the beautiful things around them and sharing the magic of this special place.

Take it further:

- Place pupils into small groups and invite them to work together to build a secret place. You might choose to do this initially by making models using card and paper.

- Next see what kind of creations your class can make using chairs and tables and large pieces of material. Get each group of pupils to build a place where they will feel calm and tranquil, hidden away from the rest of the world.

- Ask pupils to think hard about how to create a tranquil environment in the structure they are building. What would make it feel secret and shut off from the world? How do you enter? And how much room does it need inside?

- Once the building is complete get pupils to invite others into their secret place, describing how it is special to them.

- Play various types of music to pupils and see which one they would like to hear when they are in their secret place – which music makes them feel calm and which music makes them feel excited?

If spirituality were a picture, it would be iceberg blue with faded yellow puzzle like pieces floating aimlessly around. If spirituality was a sound, it would be a barely audible echo carried by the wind. If spirituality was a person, it would be a shy and graceful yet playful child.

Ross Bolwell-Williams

Source of stories on the spirit, making wishes and tales of wisdom

http:talesofwisdom.com

Burnett, G. *Mrs Ockleton's Rainbow Kite and Other Tales: The Anthology*, Carmarthen: Crown House, 2006.

Owen, N. *More Magic of Metaphor: Stories for Leaders, Influencers, Motivators and Spiral Dynamics Wizards*, Carmarthen: Crown House, 2004.

Owen, N. *The Magic of Metaphor: 77 Stories for Teachers, Trainers and Thinkers*, Carmarthen: Crown House, 2001.

Owen N. *The Salmon of Knowledge: Stories for Work, Life, the Dark Shadow and Oneself*, Carmarthen: Crown House, 2009.

Wright, *A. Storytelling with Children*, Oxford: Oxford University Press, 1995.

Bibliography

Boa, F. *The Way of Myth: Talking with Joseph Campbell*, Boston and London: Shambala, 1994.

Bowkett, S. *For the Moon There is the Cloud: Stories in the Zen Tradition*, London: Collins Educational, 1996.

Bowkett, S. *Dojen the Wanderer*, Stafford: Network Educational Press, 2004.

Bowkett, S. *StoryMaker Catch Pack: Using genre fiction as a resource for accelerated learning*, Stafford: Network Educational Press, 2004.

Bowkett, S. and Stanley, S. *But Why? Developing philosophical thinking in the classroom*, Stafford: Network Educational Press, 2004.

Dawkins, R. *The God Delusion*, London: Black Swan, 2007.

Dossey, L. *Healing Beyond the Body*, London: Piatkus, 2009.

Egan, K. *The Educated Mind: How Cognitive Tools Shape Our Understanding*, Chicago: University of Chicago Press, 1997.

Feldman, C. and Kornfield, J. (eds) *Stories of the Spirit, Stories of the Heart: parables of the spiritual path from around the world*, San Francisco, CA: HarperCollins, 1991.

Gardner, H. *Multiple Intelligences*, New Horizons, 2006.

Honoré, C. *In Praise of Slow*, London: Orion, 2005.

Kubler-Ross, E. *On Death and Dying*, London: Routledge, 1969.

Law, S. *The Philosophy Files 1*, London: Orion, 2000.

Law, S. *The Philosophy Files 2*, London: Orion, 2003.

Long, B. *Meditation: a foundation course*, London: Barry Long Foundation, 1992.

Manley Hopkins, G. *Poems and Prose*, ed. W. H. Gardner, Harmondsworth: Penguin, 1970.

Ozaniec, N. *101 Essential Tips: Everyday Meditation*, London: Dorling Kindersley, 1997.

Postman, N. and Weingartner, C. *Teaching as a Subversive Activity*, Harmondsworth: Penguin, 1972.

Propp, V. *Morphology of the Folktale*, Austin, TX: University of Texas Press, 2001.

Radin, D. *The Conscious Universe: The Scientific Truth of Psychic Phenomena*, San Francisco, CA: HarperCollins, 2009.

Reps, P. *Zen Flesh, Zen Bones*, Harmondsworth: Penguin, 1980.

Shigematsu, S. *A Zen Harvest: Japanese Folk Zen Sayings (Haiku, Dodoitsu, and Waka)*, New York and Tokyo, Weatherhill, 1992.

Schiller, D. *The Little Zen Companion*, New York: Workman Publishing, 1994.

Smith, M. J. *When I Say No, I Feel Guilty*, New York: Bantam Books, 1975.

Stryk, L. (trans.) *On Love and Barley*: *Haiku of Basho*, Harmondsworth: Penguin, 1985.

Thomas, R. S. *Selected Poems 1946–1968*, London: Granada Publishing, 1973.

Watts, A. *Tao: the watercourse way*, Harmondsworth: Penguin, 1981.

Watts, A. *What Is Zen?* CA: New World Library, 2000.

Williams, M. *The Velveteen Rabbit*, New York: Doubleday, 1958.

Resources
CD Content

Tales to Tell
   1 Tales to Tell.pdf contains 4 quotes supplied as separate A4 posters

Saying Goodbye
   2. Saying Goodbye.pdf contains the illustration supplied as an A4 poster

Koan, Koan – Gone!
   3 Koan Koan Gone.pdf contains the illustration supplied as an A4 poster

The Harp of Dagda
   4 The Harp of Dagda.pdf contains the illustration supplied as an A4 poster
   5 The Harp of Dagda.pdf contains a worksheet

As One Door Closes
   6 As One Door Closes.pdf contains the illustration supplied as an A4 poster

A Story of Circles
   7 A Story of Circles.pdf contains 2 illustrations supplied as A4 posters

The Endless Story
   8 The Endless Story.pdf contains the illustration supplied as an A4 poster and worksheet

Once Upon a Time There Was a Giant
   9 Once Upon a Time There Was a Giant.pdf contains the story and illustration available as an A4 poster

Story Mapping
   10 Story Mapping.pdf contains the illustration supplied as an A4 poster

Looking from Another Angle
   11 Looking from Another Angle.pdf contains a photograph marked up and supplied as an A4 poster
   12 Looking from Another Angle.pdf contains a Spirituality cloudscape worksheet
   13 Looking from Another Angle.pdf contains a worksheet

Moral Obligation
   14 Moral Obligation.pdf contains a worksheet

Harmony and Discord
  15 Harmony and Discord.pdf contains 2 keyboard illustrations supplied as A4 posters

The World Is Wiggly but Not Wobbly
  16 The World Is Wiggly but Not Wobbly.pdf contains a worksheet
  17 The World Is Wiggly but Not Wobbly.pdf contains the Yun-Men quote supplied as an A4 poster

Wu Wei
  18 Wu Wei.pdf contains the Wu Wei worksheet

Truth or Lie
  19 Truth or Lie.pdf contains a worksheet

Yes, but Where's the Proof?
  20 Yes but Wheres the Proof.pdf contains the figure available as printable cards

The Well
  21 The Well.pdf contains the illustration available as an A4 poster
  22 The Well.pdf contains a worksheet

The Backwards Walking Man
  23 The Backwards Walking Man.pdf contains the illustration supplied as an A4 poster

A Time for Everything
  24 A Time for Everything.pdf contains the Bible passage supplied as an A4 poster
  25 A Time for Everything.pdf contains a worksheet

A Boy Ate a Chocolate Biscuit
  26 A Boy Ate a Chocolate Biscuit.pdf contains the story and illustration supplied as an A4 poster

Guided Fantasy
  27 Guided Fantasy.pdf contains the meditation script

Conflict Statues
  28 Conflict Statues.pdf contains the actions available as a printable card

Moral Minitales
  29 Moral Minitales.pdf contains a worksheet

Would You Rather …?
  30 Would You Rather.pdf contains a worksheet

The Mundane and the Sacred
  31 The Mundane and the Sacred.pdf contains the 2 lists supplied as A4 posters

First Light
  32 First Light.pdf contains the illustration supplied as an A4 poster

33 First Light.pdf contains pictures of Earth from space/earthquakes/birds in flight/ lightning
34 First Light.pdf contains a worksheet

There's Nothing There
35 There's Nothing There.pdf contains the illustration supplied as an A4 poster

The Ladybirds
36 The Ladybirds.pdf contains the illustration supplied as an A4 poster
37 The Ladybirds.pdf contains a worksheet

Once There Was a Unicorn
38 One There Was a Unicorn.pdf contains the story and illustration as an A4 poster

How Do You Bury a Rainbow?
39 How Do You Bury a Rainbow.pdf contains the illustration supplied as an A4 poster
40 How Do You Bury a Rainbow.pdf contains a worksheet

I Wonder Why?
41 I Wonder Why.pdf contains the poem displayed as an A4 poster
42 I Wonder Why.pdf contains a worksheet

I Wonder
43 I Wonder.pdf contains a worksheet
44 I Wonder.pdf contains the Einstein quote displayed as an A4 poster

Looking at Symbols
45 Looking at Symbols.pdf contains 2 illustrations supplied as A4 posters
46 Looking at Symbols.pdf contains a worksheet
47 Looking at Symbols.pdf contains the numbered table as an A4 poster

Prayer Flags
48 Prayer Flags.pdf contains a worksheet

This Is Me
49 This Is Me.pdf contains the illustration supplied as an A4 poster
50 This Is Me.pdf contains an A4 poster of an elaborate blank picture frame

Divine Inspiration
51 Divine Inspiration.pdf contains the hymn displayed as an A4 poster

Once Upon a Time There Was a Girl
52 One Upon a Time There Was a Girl.pdf contains the story and illustration supplied as an A4 poster

Natural Curiosity
53 Natural Curiosity.pdf contains an A4 poster of the questions

Playing with Words
54 Playing with Words.pdf contains the proverb displayed as an A4 poster

Myku
55 Myku.pdf contains the poems displayed as an A4 poster

A Moon on Water
56 A Moon on Water.pdf contains the cover image A4 poster
57 A Moon on Water.pdf contains the poems displayed as an A4 poster
58 A Moon on Water.pdf contains the folk sayings displayed as an A4 poster

Screen Savers
59 Screen Savers.pdf contains the illustration displayed as an A4 poster
60 Screen Savers.pdf contains a worksheet

A Secret Place
61 A Secret Place.pdf contains a worksheet

Audio CD Listing

Tr	Story	Writer	Narrator	Music	Timing
1	A Moon on Water – Haiku	Steve	Eleanor	Emily	2.39
2	Saying Goodbye	Roy	Roy	Emily	5.31
3	The Harp of Dagda	Tim	Tim	Tim	2.53
4	As One Door closes	Tim	Tim	Tim	3.50
5	A Story of Circles	Steve	Steve	Emily	8.06
6	Story Mapping (The Day the Sun Refused to Set)	Trisha	Trisha	Emily	4.20
7	The Well	Roy	Roy	Emily	9.01
8	The Backwards Walking Man	Steve	Trisha	Emily	4.10
9	A Matter of Choice	Steve	Steve	Emily	3.18
10	A Time for Everything	Tim	Tim	Tim	3.21
11	A Boy Ate a Chocolate Biscuit –	Trisha	Roy	Emily	0.41
12	First Light	Roy	Roy	Emily	6.47
13	There's Nothing There	Tim	Tim	Emily	2.59
14	The Ladybirds	Steve	Steve	Emily	3.25
15	I Wonder Why	Tim	Charlotte, Eleanor, Tim		2.29
16	This Is Me	Roy	Trisha	Charlotte	10.30
17	Caedmon's Hymn	Tim	Tim	Tim	0.59
18	Do Your own Thing	Tim	Tim	Eleanor Charlotte Tim	3.18
19	Once Upon a Time There Was a Girl	Trisha	Trisha	Tim	0.52